POINTS

The Most Practical Program Ever
to Improve Your Self-Image

David A. Gustafson

Blue Dolphin Publishing

Published by Blue Dolphin Publishing, Inc.
P.O. Box 1908, Nevada City, CA 95959

ISBN: 0-931892-74-0

Library of Congress Cataloging-In-Publication Data

Gustafson, David A., 1946–
    Points : the most practical program ever to improve
your self-image / David A. Gustafson.
    192 p.   cm.
    Includes bibliographical references.
    ISBN 0-931892-74-0 : $12.95
    1. Self-perception.   2. Success—Psychological aspects.
I. Title.
BF697.5.S43G87 1992
158'.1—dc20   92-5016
                                                  CIP

Printed in the United States of America by
Blue Dolphin Press, Inc., Grass Valley, California

10   9   8   7   6   5   4   3   2   1

Very sensible and very promising without any lofty claims. . . . Points may define the approach to self-improvement for the 90s.

Tom Billingsley
Musician, composer

Dave's work inspired me more than anyone or anything in a very long time. I believe this book offers a formula which, if followed, will absolutely guarantee success for everyone.

Doug Pajak
Sales consultant and trainer

This book should be required reading—not only for every high school and college student, but for every parent as well.

Ronald Lee Anderson
Vice-president FPII International

POINTS

If American business leaders followed the principles identified in this book, we would once again become the dominant world economic power. If America's government leaders followed the principles identified in this book, our political system would be cleaned up overnight. If America's citizens followed the principles identified in this book, we would finally all live in paradise.

Bob Levene
International attorney

While other self-help books offer a spiritual get-rich quick scheme, Points *is more a guide to prudent investing.*

Darren Lott
Conceptual analyst, actor, triathlete,
master scuba instructor, black belt

Dedication

To my father

Arthur R. Gustafson

1917-1992

Table of Contents

Acknowledgments

I wonder if anyone ever reads the acknowledgments section of a book other than those who think their name may be included. However, there are a number of people who are very important to me and who I hope get the opportunity to read this and know I love them.

Ron Anderson for being my best friend when it was very important to have one.

Homer Braggins for being my friend and for nurturing me as only he could.

Bob and Ellie Cardoff for helping me get started.

Laurinda Cook-Ericson for being there when the page was blank.

To the FPH (Ron Anderson, Tom Anderson, and Tony
Bukoski) for a whole number of reasons.

Cathy Freeman for her sincere desire to see me and this book
do well.

Sharon Ginther for her enthusiastic support.

Lisa Haggard for having loved and believed in me and for
being the catalyst for a new beginning.

Bob Harrer for being there when all this began, for supporting me through the most difficult growth phase, and for offering the healing laughter.

Al Johnson for helping me to explore my past.

Gene Karczewski for being a true friend and a true gentleman. He is a man of integrity and dignity who deserves all
the best of life.

Jim Leonard for always being there.

Bob Levene for his sage comments and encouragement.

To my "Master Mind Group" for more reasons than I can even
list.

Vicki McCarthy for her encouragement and her sincere desire
to grow. I enjoy watching her blossom.

Mike Miller for sharing his experience, strength, and hope.

Jerry Nanni for the years of friendship.

Kirk Scarborough for caring enough to listen to my advice.

Joyce Simpson for listening and guiding.

To the members of Team Steele (Carl Beehler, Joe Benjamin, Tom Billingsley, Ray Hight, Kent and Linda Kochheiser, Lori Lee, and Darren Lott) for the opportunity to expand my comfort zone.

Sue Vranna for gaining points with her positive lifestyle and for enjoying the benefits of the quality life she so richly deserves.

Carole Waggoner for the many hours of sharing and caring conversations.

To my parents and brothers and sisters for loving me and supporting me in my journey as only they can.

1

Self-Image and Success

SOME PEOPLE FACE LIFE HEAD ON, accepting whatever comes and relishing the challenge, while others slink through the shadows trying not to be noticed. Some enjoy happiness, prosperity, and love; others appear condemned to misery, poverty, ridicule, and scorn. In short, some light a candle, while others curse the darkness.

Is life so unfair to bless a few, then curse and revile the rest? No. The universe does not have favorites. Despite all appearances, there is an orderliness to life. Each human being has the opportunity to achieve any goal. The limitations of poverty, ill health, lack of education, and prejudice can be overcome. There are no absolute roadblocks to success; there are only challenges.

You, like every other person, are equipped with the ability to change your life. You have been provided with a mind that is so powerful it can change the world. Psychologist William James wrote, "The greatest discovery of my generation is that human beings, by changing the inner attitudes of their minds, can change the outer aspects of their lives" (James, 1980). If you live under conditions which are unacceptable, don't try to change these external conditions; instead put your effort into changing yourself and your attitudes. Your world will improve the moment you are ready for it.

At first, this concept may not make sense. How can you possibly affect your environment by what you are thinking? It seems too simple, but it is not. The only way you can possibly achieve success is to first prepare yourself to accept success. If you continually grouse and complain, you only reinforce the negative. To become a winner, you must first think like a winner.

For most of us it is not easy to become a success, even after we accept and practice this philosophy. We cannot simply say, "Okay, I'll think good thoughts and tomorrow I'll be rich." If you are like me, you must transform your fundamental self-image in order to be successful. It is not enough to want to succeed; you must also feel worthy of it. To *become* a winner, you must first believe yourself to *be* one within the depths of your subconscious mind.

I know. I have tried to achieve what I believed to be success through many means. I have read scores of books and listened to hundreds of hours of tapes which offered guidelines to wealth and prosperity. I have sought happiness and *the answer* in seminars, training, lectures, retreats, and encounters. These exercises had one thing in common—each dramatically changed my life for about fifteen minutes!

No matter which courses I undertook or books I read, I seemed unable to achieve any promised breakthrough to success. During these studies, my income rose gradually, my social life improved somewhat, and I did feel better about myself, but I never did discover the treasured secrets for vast wealth, love, and happiness. Nevertheless, I continued in my pursuit. After all, my life was improving somewhat even while my wallet was becoming less of a strain to carry.

In *Think and Grow Rich*, Napoleon Hill (1960) boldly stated, "Whatever THE MIND OF MAN can CONCEIVE and BELIEVE it can ACHIEVE." I read the book and was inspired. Together with a friend, who had also read the book, I conceived a plan for a large and profitable empire. We founded a corporation dedicated to providing affordable computers to homes and small businesses. After he resigned due to a family crisis, I continued the operation. In less than a year I guided the company to where we were about to become a major factor in the marketplace. We had visions of a public stock offering and great wealth. Our financial consultant told me, "Dave, you are guaranteed to become a millionaire. Just stay out of your own way and everything will be fine."

I could not stay out of my own way however, and the business failed. Even today it is easy for me to blame external conditions. IBM entered the personal computer market and sent a number of companies like mine out of business. There was a recession, so fewer people had the discretionary income to purchase our products. Our suppliers were unable to deliver in a timely manner, due to their own financial problems. All of these reasons are true, but they do not account for my failure. Other similar businesses adjusted to the changes and prospered. Ours did not. I simply did not reach my goal and, at the time, I did not know why.

Napoleon Hill had said that the human mind could achieve whatever it could conceive and believe. I possessed a human mind and I could certainly conceive of being a millionaire. After all, hadn't I founded the company, wrote the business plan, hired the staff, and interested the investors? My concepts were sound and solid, and we did succeed for a time. What then was there that prevented me from achieving the success promised by Dr. Hill and others? I pondered that question for a long time.

Eventually, I realized that my failure wasn't due to my inability to conceive of success. Therefore, it must be due to my lack of capacity to believe I deserved it. No matter how I tried, I could not believe myself worthy of achieving my lofty goals.

All of the books, tapes, and classes had failed to instill in me the one essential ingredient to success—how to believe in myself. They talked of a positive mental attitude, goal setting, letting go of fear and guilt, and hundreds of other concepts that are valuable and make sense. What they did not say, or more correctly what I did not understand, was how I could change my innermost self to believe that I am a winner.

Belief and Success

There is but a single condition which dictates whether one will enjoy happiness, prosperity, and success, or wallow in failure, poverty, and misery. It is a basic law of the universe, and is as true for the native living in a primitive hut as it is for a king in his palace. There is no way to avoid this law, no way to cheat it, no way to repeal it.

This law, which dictates our condition in life and determines the paths we take, is very simple. It has been stated in various ways for centuries. The New Testament of the Bible discloses this law several times. In Mark 9:23 it is stated as: "All things are possible to him who believes." In Matthew 17:20 the law is written: "If you have faith as a grain of mustard seed, you will say to this mountain, 'Move from here to there,' and it will move; and *nothing will be impossible to you.*"

William James, the psychologist cited earlier wrote, "Belief at the beginning of a doubtful undertaking is the one thing that will guarantee the success of any venture" (James, 1980).

Norman Vincent Peale, the proponent of positive thinking, contends: "Failure begins in your thoughts when you hold the idea that you are actually incapable, that you are born to lose. So to counteract failure, develop the ability to believe. Tell yourself in no uncertain terms, 'I was born to be a winner.' To be that, you will just have to be a believer because winners are always believers. Losers are never real believers" (Peale, 1986).

The 1969 New York Mets motto was, "You Gotta Believe," and it spurred them to win the World Series.

This principle can be stated very simply so it will be easy to remember. Write it in big letters and tape it to your bathroom mirror and on your refrigerator door. Imprint it in your mind, for it affects your life:

WE GET WHAT WE BELIEVE WE DESERVE

You may argue that external conditions have a great deal to do with what happens to you. You may also assert that there are other influences such as the basic talents and attributes you were given by nature. Without a doubt these factors have an influence on your life for they contribute to your attitude of success or failure. However, every external condition, talent, or personal attribute can be overcome or used to advantage through your basic beliefs about yourself and your world. In other words, you are able to accomplish whatever it is that your self-image accepts as appropriate for you.

A trait common in many people is blaming outside influences for their failures. To blame or credit outside influences or even natural gifts is merely to use excuses to abrogate responsibility for your own life. Of course there are thousands of stories of failure due to external conditions. It is easier to blame your setbacks on something outside of yourself than it is to accept total and undiluted responsibility for your own life. The primary difference between winners and losers is in their perception. Winners perceive themselves as being in control of their lives; losers view themselves as victims. Winners take responsibility; losers blame others.

It is not a conscious choice to be a winner or a loser. Rather the belief resides within your subconscious. Most people would consciously prefer to be successful. They may be very vague about their personal definition of success, have no idea of how to go about achieving success, and may not understand how to define goals. Nevertheless, almost everyone consciously desires a higher quality life.

It is your subconscious mind which either prevents you from achieving your goals or impels you to success. In many instances it even obstructs you from setting viable goals. Your subconscious stores your self-image which, in turn, dictates the course of your life. While it is possible to override this mechanism for a short time through conscious will power, the subconscious self-image will always prevail. It is this self-image which either pilots you to success or dictates your failure.

Talent and natural ability are not guarantees of success. In fact, we often waste and abuse those very gifts which have been bestowed on us so freely. Your success is directly attributable to the degree to which you believe you deserve it. There are thousands of stories of those who overcame adversity to succeed because they believed they could. Beethoven was deaf; Jackie Robinson was black; Lincoln was raised in poverty, had little formal education, and lost every major election he was in until he became President.

These people certainly could blame external conditions for their failures. Instead they achieved greatness. Helen Keller could easily have surrendered to her handicaps and no one would blame her. After all she was blind, deaf, and dumb. Yet she achieved greatness and contributed much to society—more than most people blessed with a great many more advantages.

Each of these people had one thing in common: THEY BELIEVED IN THEMSELVES. They believed that it was their right to succeed. They believed they deserved to win and would accept nothing less. Edison attempted a thousand experiments before he finally invented the light bulb. He could have abandoned the project and explained that conditions were not appropriate. Yet he knew he could succeed, and that made it impossible for him to fail.

The Components of Self-image

There is a direct correlation between self-image and success. To repeat once again: WE GET WHAT WE BELIEVE WE DESERVE. Winners believe they deserve success; losers feel unworthy of it. Winners win and losers lose based on their self-image. Are you a winner? Evaluate yourself. Determine the quality of your life for it more accurately confirms your self-image than any other possible measurement.

Your self-image is a product of all of your experiences and resides in the subconscious mind. The subconscious mind is a storehouse of all the messages it has received since birth and before. It does not contain an editor and therefore accepts any messages it receives. If you send it a message that you are a loser, the subconscious will accept it and impel you to act accordingly. Losers lose. Therefore, the next time an opportunity arises to win or lose, the subconscious will know that you are a loser and will force you to do whatever is required to affirm your loser status. The subconscious does not evaluate whether losing is less desirable than winning—remember that it has no editor. It only reacts in a manner consistent with its programmed image.

Your subconscious has received millions of messages that in summary build your self-image. Each time you tell yourself you are stupid or inferior, your subconscious stores the data as fact. If others insult you or offer negative criticism, your conscious mind, which possesses an editor, has the opportunity to accept or deny the truth of such information. If such a declaration is accepted as true, it enters the subconscious as one more loser message. A negative statement from another can be denied by the conscious mind and replaced with a positive statement such as, "He is wrong, I am very intelligent." In such a situation the subconscious mind will receive and store a winner message.

The number of winner messages minus the number of loser messages creates the equation for a positive or negative self-image. If you have accumulated more winner messages than loser messages, you will have a positive self-image and will find a way to win regardless of the external circumstances.

Points

When I was a child, I had an image of God as a wizened old man with a long flowing white beard, clad in a dazzling white robe and wearing leather sandals. He carried a ledger book, and in it recorded my every action and thought. When I was good, He awarded me points. If I sinned, He took them away. I believed that when I died, God would allow me into heaven only if I had accumulated enough points. If I fell short of the necessary quota, He would condemn me to hell. To me, God was but an Omnipotent Scorekeeper.

I no longer hold this image of God, but instead believe that it closely depicts the workings of the subconscious mind. Your subconscious acts as a personal scorekeeper, tallying points for every action or thought. There is one major difference between the image of God as a scorekeeper and the image of the subconscious as one. With the subconscious mechanism, you need not wait until you die to know heaven or hell. If you have enough points, life is heaven on earth. If you suffer a deficit, it can be hell.

Each act you perform and each thought you entertain has a point value which is determined by your conscious mind and stored in your subconscious. It is obvious that how you act or react affects the present. What is important for you to understand is that the points associated with the action also dictate your future by affecting your self-image. Ralph Waldo Emerson describes this concept in his essay, "Compensation": "Cause and effect, means and ends, seed and fruit, cannot be severed; for the effect already blooms in the cause, the end preexists in the means, the fruit in the seed."

What Emerson is saying is that you dictate your future by what you do in the present. The Bible agrees. In Galatians 6:7 it is written: ". . . for whatever a man sows, that he will also reap." If you plant positive thoughts and deeds, you will harvest a quality life. You decide your future by what you do in the present.

In Buddhism this concept is called karma. Alan Watts (1957) describes karma as, "consequential action," which means that there is a result or consequence to everything we do.

To Hugh Prather, understanding this concept is a sign of maturity. He writes:

One element of maturity is the realization that we don't get away with anything. Any advantage gained or convenience taken, any private procrastination or insincerity, no matter how subtle or quick in passing, is paid for. Not dramatically. Often not noticeably. But enough that we learn, eventually, it is not worth it (Prather, 1977).

Building the Self-Image

Every event, action, and thought either improves or detracts from your self-image by adding or subtracting points. In order to achieve and maintain a winner's self-image, you must continually add positive messages to improve your self-image and to offset any existing negative messages. If we were to assign point values to positive messages and negative messages, we could say that we must send our subconscious more points than we subtract if we are to be winners. The formula for self-image then becomes:

POINTS GAINED MINUS POINTS LOST = SELF-IMAGE

This formula demonstrates why there can be no sudden change in self-image. It requires quite some time to accumulate the points to improve your self-image enough to enable you to achieve your goals and ambitions. Of course, such growth can be achieved, and the results will be remarkable. Once your self-esteem is high enough, you will easily attain the wealth, health, happiness, and love you now desire. Through your actions you can change your insides, which will have the effect of making your external world better.

Beware of trying to change too rapidly. It can only lead to failure and disappointment. You will lose more points than you gain. For example, suppose that you have the self-image that you are lazy. This self-image has been cultivated during a lifetime of your conscious mind sending, "I am lazy" messages to your subconscious. You may have heard messages such as, "You never clean your room, you're the laziest kid I know," and "Your work is sloppy because you're so lazy." Perhaps you have said, "I don't want to get up and go to work today. I feel too lazy." Each time you accepted one of these messages, it costs you ambition points. By now you may have a severe deficit.

One day you decide to become physically fit. You decide to arise an hour earlier each morning and jog a mile. The first day you are up with the alarm and out the door. You trot, run and stumble your way for most of a mile and return home exhilarated with such a marvelous sense of accomplishment that you renew your resolve to do this every day. Your conscious mind and alleged will power have overridden your self-image of laziness. You have even gained a few ambition points to offset your deficit.

The next day you awaken quite stiff and sore from your prior day's adventure. You still get up, but somewhat more slowly. This day you stagger around the track, all the while feeling sorry for yourself. With each agonizing step you remember that you could still be warmly secure in bed like the rest of the family. You are sure that no one appreciates your efforts anyhow!

You may continue in your agony for a few more days, until eventually you decide to sleep later and forego this morning torture. Soon you have gone several weeks without jogging. When you think about it, you rationalize that you are just too busy to undertake anything so ambitious as self-improvement. What you are really telling your subconscious is that you are just too lazy to pursue physical fitness. Your negative self-image undermined you one more time. Not only that, you now actually have a greater point deficit as a result of the messages you sent your subconscious during this latest failure.

No matter how consciously willful you may be, you can not overcome the power of your subconscious. Eventually it will take control and cause you to act in a manner consistent with the image it holds of you. You must learn to re-program it.

If, instead of creating a situation in which you were doomed to fail, you understood that you must first gain self-esteem points, you could have succeeded. Instead of trying to get up an hour earlier and jogging a mile, you start more slowly by walking on your lunch break for a few weeks, gradually increasing the distance. Soon you jog two days a week and continue walking on the remaining days. While you are exercising, you recite affirmations to your fitness. At the same time you set a definite goal for fitness and spend time each day visualizing its achievement. Eventually you are able to compensate for your point deficit. Within a short time you arise with the sun each morning and easily jog several miles. You are now enjoying yourself, feeling fit, and accumulating points daily.

The subconscious tallies each and every point it is sent and knows precisely if you are in the positive or have a deficit. As we will see in the next chapter, every event has a built-in point value associated with it. There are no neutral events. Everything you do each and every day provides the opportunity to gain self-esteem points or to lose them.

My Quest for Points

What has happened in my life since I have undertaken the challenge of improving my self-image by accumulating points? I have dedicated my life to practicing this philosophy and to training others to do the same. The formula works. I know, for I have seen hundreds of examples of remarkable improvements in self-esteem and quality of life.

In my situation, I believe that I had a further distance to travel than most of the people I counsel and train in this philosophy. By my estimate, I began my quest with a severe deficit. I was raised in a less than nurturing environment and did nothing to improve my self-image after I left home. I was divorced, smoked two packs of cigarettes a day, drank excessively, suffered high blood pressure, was overweight, rarely exercised, was sloppy in my appearance and surroundings, and worked at a job I despised.

One day I did a quick evaluation of the condition of my life and found it wanting. My life held very little value for me. This was indeed a crisis point in my life. I could either drop out entirely or attempt to improve.

Fortunately, I made a conscious decision to better myself and my condition. I began by studying self-help books and self-improvement tapes, and attended growth classes. I even joined a support group dedicated to encouraging people like me to improve the quality of our lives.

Because I did not know the concept of points, I was still disappointed when I did not achieve the dramatic changes promised me as a result of these self-improvement attempts. I have said earlier that each self-help program changed my life dramatically for about fifteen minutes. While that is true, they did actually serve a greater function. Even though I did not realize it at the time, each book, tape, and course added a few points to my long-suffering self-image.

Eventually I gathered enough self-esteem points to quit my job and start a small business. By providing quality service, I gained enough points from that experience to form the corporation discussed earlier.

That was too ambitious an undertaking. I had yet to acquire enough points to succeed at running a large corporation. However, I gained something valuable from the entire experience. As a result of the research and analysis of my business setback, I began to understand the concept of points. Once the understanding awakened within me, I could see how I often sabotaged my success. I was not taking care of myself physically, emotionally, or spiritually; I looked for an edge wherever I could take one, and I often found fault with others rather than accepting responsibility for my life.

This book is dedicated to telling you how I, and hundreds of others with whom I have worked, have used the concept of points to improve our lives. The information presented is always based on our actual experiences of applying this timeless wisdom. Everything I tell you has been proven to work.

Since I began to actively accumulate points, my life has improved in every area. I am very happy with the results so far, and know that it will only get better. My income, which is derived exclusively from helping others, is ten times greater than that of just a few years ago. I was once terrified of crowds; now I enjoy speaking before audiences of any size.

Material goods have been bestowed upon me and I enjoy my accomplishments. I exercise regularly and feel trim and healthy. In fact I feel ten years younger than I did ten years ago. I rarely eat junk food and no longer smoke cigarettes or drink alcohol. Where once I was a loner, I now have several dear friends whom I love and who love me. We have a trust and an honesty that can only come from a secure relationship. I am able to give to others and contribute to their well-being.

I am close to my family and share in their lives. Those emotions I would not allow myself to experience, such as love, caring, and giving, now offer me deep satisfaction. I even allow myself to feel sadness, sorrow, and pain, for they also demonstrate

I am fully alive. I no longer have to hide in the shadows. I relish life and all that it offers.

All of this and more can happen for you. Winners win and losers lose. Take the time to build a winning self-image, and it will be easy for you to succeed. You can enjoy a good life just by leading a good life and believing in yourself. If you have low self-esteem and want to avoid even more negativity, or if you are blessed with a surplus of positive points and desire even more abundance, this book will show you how to improve your self-image a point at a time.

CHAPTER SUMMARY

1. WE GET WHAT WE BELIEVE WE DESERVE.

2. The self-image is based on a summary of every action and thought you have ever had. The positive improves your self-image, the negative detracts from it.

3. Every event results in positive or negative messages being sent to your subconscious. The subconscious tallies these messages and adds them to the messages already stored. You either receive points or lose them. The self-image is the sum of these points:

   POSITIVE POINTS MINUS NEGATIVE POINTS
   EQUALS SELF-IMAGE

4. Winners win and losers lose. If you have a winning self-image, you will generally find a way to win. If you lose more than you win, improve your self-image and you will reverse this curse.

2

Self-Image and Points

YOUR SELF-IMAGE IS A VERY POWERFUL ENTITY. From it, you actually create your own reality. You determine your successes and your failures. You dictate to other people exactly how they are to treat you. Your self-image is your window through which you view the world and through which you allow the world to view you. Sound farfetched? Not at all. In fact this concept is the essence of a successful and happy life.

Once you accept and understand the philosophy that YOU GET WHAT YOU BELIEVE YOU DESERVE, you can proceed to improve the quality of your life. Unless you are willing to take responsibility for your actions, you are condemned to live as a victim and will never fully know success or happiness.

Your self-image determines what it is you believe you deserve. It resides in the subconscious mind. "The subconscious mind operates as a storehouse of past knowledge, observations, and conclusions" (Brandon, 1969). Your subconscious self-image compels you to act and react in a manner consistent with the beliefs it holds. If you have a healthy self-image, you will generally conduct yourself accordingly. You will avoid destructive behavior and will instead comport yourself in a way which enhances your self-image.

Your self-image is comprised of every message your subconscious has ever received. These messages may be positive and enhance your self-image, or they may be negative and detract from it. To reiterate from the last chapter: The self-image is the sum of points gained minus those lost. You have self-esteem when your self-image is positive; you have self-loathing when it is negative.

Your Self-Image Acts like a Thermostat

Your self-image is your personal definition of you. It is the sum of every belief you hold about yourself, and as such, it dictates the treatment you believe you deserve. You refuse to accept less than is your perceived due, and you reject all overtures to grant you more. In that way, your self-image acts like a thermostat for the quality of your life. Pay you too little, and your thermostat will kick in and you'll soon find another job; pay you too much, and your thermostat will cool you to the point you'll find a non-productive way to dispose of the excess.

Your self-image controls your demeanor and your actions which demonstrate to others exactly how they are to deal with you. If, in your opinion, someone treats you poorly, you refuse to accept this behavior. You let him know in direct or subtle ways that such treatment is not acceptable. He will either alter his dealing with you or you will alter the relationship. The same concept rings true when someone concedes you better treatment than you believe you deserve. You become suspicious, wary, and defensive. "What does she want from me? What are her motives?" you ask yourself. Soon you withdraw or demonstrate your discomfort and distrust for such favorable treatment. Eventually the other person reads your clues and adjusts her approach.

At what level is your thermostat set now? You can easily tell by observing your level of comfort in various situations. For example, watch your reactions in a restaurant. If the service is poor, do you tolerate it and assume that it is indicative of the quality to be expected these days? If the service is great, do you tell yourself the waiter is only fishing for a big tip?

A direct benefit of a healthier self-image is an increase in your thermostat threshold. The range and settings for your thermostat dictate your comfort zone. As you feel better and better about yourself, you will expect and enjoy a higher quality of life, and you will broaden your comfort zone.

Your Self-Image Is a Signal to Others

Your self-image loudly proclaims to the world how you expect to be treated. Remember when you were a child and as a joke someone would pen "KICK ME" on a piece of paper and surreptitiously tape it to another student's back? Until he figured it out, the victim couldn't understand why people were kicking him. As adults we also seem to wear such signs, but we place them on ourselves, thanks to our self-image. Our signs proclaim: "I have no sense of humor," "Love me, then leave me," "I hate my job, but I need the money," or "Tease me so I can get angry." Others read these signs and treat us accordingly. In turn we become hurt, angry, or depressed. How dare they? Yet the fault lies within us. We tell them exactly how we wish to be treated, then act amazed when they oblige.

Hopefully you have a more positive self-image. Your sign will proclaim loudly and clearly: "I DESERVE RESPECT," "I AM LOVABLE," or "I ENJOY LIFE." As you improve your self-image, your sign becomes clearer and more positive. You believe you deserve more and so indicate it to yourself and the world.

Observe others to see their signs. Have you ever noticed a person who always gets first-class service? His sign may say: "I EXPECT THE BEST." Do you have a friend to whom you can confide your hopes and fears? Perhaps her sign proclaims: "I AM WARM AND SINCERE." Do you know someone with a sign: "I AM A STRONG LEADER?" How do people react to her?

Do you know what sign you wear? Sure you do. Just observe how others are treating you. Look at the quality and quantity of your friends. Evaluate how your boss and co-workers deal with you. See how your spouse and children react to you. If you're not married and wish you were, what sign do you carry which prevents you from attracting a suitable mate?

How can you change your sign? In other words, how can you be, do, and have more? The answer is simple though the implementation is not: change your self-image. You have the power. You have the potential. You have available more capacity than you will ever be able to use during this lifetime. Forget your limitations, for they are merely imagined. Realize instead that you have boundless opportunity. You have a strength of body and a power of mind far beyond any challenge you may encounter. The only limitation you have is the belief that you have limitations.

You are determining your future at this very moment. Your thoughts and actions are modifying your self-image, and your self-image is the basic determinant of your potential and your perceived limitations. Focus on your shortcomings and they will dominate your life. Concentrate on your strengths and they will multiply.

There Are No Limits

The newspapers are filled with remarkable demonstrations of human potential and achievement. Read the sports pages for some dramatic examples. In a recent Los Angeles Marathon, a man in his seventies completed the race faster than the world record of forty years before. This means senior citizens are bettering the efforts of the champions of their youth. Certainly improved nutrition and training have contributed to these remarkable advances, but the real progress is a direct result of their expanded beliefs in their abilities to perform.

Roger Bannister was the first person to run a mile in under four minutes. Until he did it, few believed it possible. Studies were conducted which "proved" that humankind had reached the limits of its potential in long distance running. The four minute mile was considered a barrier that could never be crossed.

The real barrier was not a physical one; it was the belief that there are boundaries to human accomplishment. Once Mr. Bannister accomplished his feat, several others followed. Today it is commonplace for several competitors in the same race to finish in less than four minutes. Yet there is still discussion of what the new physical limits are. Will we never learn?

Most records of physical accomplishment are only gradually improved. Rarely have there been major breakthroughs. This is because the barriers imposed by accepted beliefs are usually stretched and seldom broken. It does not have to be that way. The boundaries of human physical prowess are well beyond any levels currently perceived.

Recently, in Florida, a grandmother lifted a power pole that was crushing one of her grandchildren. Had she not acted immediately the child would have died. She saved a life through this feat of strength. Later, when reporters asked her to again lift the pole so they could take pictures, she was unable to even move it.

During the emergency, the heroine ignored her physical limitations in her desire to save a loved one. She performed a feat of strength that most would call superhuman. Once the crisis passed, her usual beliefs returned. She was once again a frail old grandmother.

This is not an isolated story. There are hundreds of incidents each year which demonstrate the same principle. Most of us use but a fraction of our brain's capacity. There are psychologists, physiologists, and other scientists who proclaim we use but a tenth of our mind's potential. Imagine having ten times the abilities you have now. What could you accomplish? The capacity is there; it is the belief in that capacity which is missing.

We are only beginning to understand the marvelous potential within each human being. Some believe we can read other's thoughts, predict the future, and move objects with our minds. We know our minds can produce pain killers without our having to ingest drugs. We can enjoy robust health and experience rapid recovery from any disease through relaxation and visualization. We could easily learn to speak several languages, memorize all the works of Shakespeare, and develop the ability to program a computer with but a few hours a week of study and practice. We could run a marathon, bicycle a hundred miles, and climb a mountain by devoting a few more hours a week to physical training. As we develop our minds and bodies, we increase our abilities to develop them even more.

The powers are there, if you choose to use them. Many of us block our potential through our negativity and our refusal to believe in our own capacities. The first step to achieving your goals is that you must believe in yourself and your power. Christ presented all of us these promises when He said, "I am come that

they might have life, and that they might have it abundantly"
(John 10:10).

Thinking versus Acting

There are two basic philosophies for self-improvement.
One school believes that you can think your way to a better way
of acting; the other believes you can act your way to a better way
of thinking. Both are correct.

Your every awareness, be it thought or action, results in a
message being sent to your subconscious. There, the message is
categorized and combined with all the similar messages which
are already stored. The outcome is either an increase or a decrease
of your self-esteem points. Positive messages increase points,
negative messages reduce them. The subconscious tallies the
points regardless of whether the original source is thought or
deed. Therefore, you can improve your life by correcting your
thinking or by bettering your actions. Preferably you will
accelerate the process by doing both.

There are no neutral events. Your every thought and act
causes you to improve or detract from your self-image. Everything you do, say, or think passes through the filter of your
conscious mind where a value is placed upon it. Your subconscious then fields the package and integrates it with all of the
other messages it has already stored. Perhaps the message is one
of triumph and victory. The subconscious applies it to the
positive side of the ledger. The message is then scored as an
improvement to your self-image, which in turn leads you to
more triumph and victory. As long as there is an abundance of
positive, you have a winning self-image. Let the negative side
gain favor, and you will find yourself creating failure and misery
in your life.

Lack of an understanding of this principle is one of the reasons many people fail to improve the quality of their lives. They may read self-help books or take improvement courses. They may learn a great deal about themselves and gain insights into their conduct. This is of little value, however, if they continue to practice all of their usual negative behavior and entertain negative thoughts. It is a form of insanity to do the same thing over and over and expect different results. To truly improve your self-image, each day you must gain more points than you lose. This means reducing negative or destructive behavior and replacing it with healthy, positive conduct. Every message received by the subconscious, regardless of the source, is stored and affects the self-image. Know your conscience and live by your principles; it is the only way to gain confidence and raise your self-esteem.

I Would If I Could

Do you find yourself incapable of taking action—even though it is in your best interest? Are you staying in a destructive relationship? Are you unable to quit a job you hate? Do you overeat and shun exercise? If you allow yourself to be mistreated or you mistreat yourself, it is because you lack self-esteem points to do otherwise. You tolerate situations, not because you enjoy them, but because you lack the self-esteem to take corrective action.

Well-intentioned friends may suggest a course of action that you know is proper, but you can't do it. Even if you deeply understand you are destroying yourself, you may be unable to stop. Something within you prevents you from starting your diet, stopping drinking, or leaving a destructive relationship.

That something is your lack of self-worth. You are unable to act in your own enlightened self-interest.

There is a way out of this destructive pattern. You can begin a course of action in which you will gain points. At first, you may not notice a change, but persist, and soon you will be able to handle situations which were once beyond you. Put into practice what you learn here, go easy on yourself when you stumble, and enjoy the fruits of having achieved high self-esteem.

How Points Are Tallied

Imagine your subconscious mind as a great scorekeeper, capable of assigning an exact score to every event in your life. Imagine also that it can instantly adjust your accumulated self-image point total to reflect the new data.

The subconscious mind does not understand nor care if the messages are positive or negative. It merely combines all the messages together to form the self-image. It does know that some offset others, much like a debit offsets a credit in double-entry bookkeeping. The subconscious believes that every message it receives is true and of value. Therefore it accepts "I am a loser" and "I am a winner" with equal interest. If it has more "I am a winner" messages stored, it believes you to be a winner and drives you to actions consistent with this image. The subconscious will react in kind for a loser's image. It simply is not aware of the desirability of one over the other. It will create whatever image your conscious mind directs, and will in turn compel you to act within the boundaries of that image.

Remember that the subconscious does no editing. It takes what it is given. In the Bible passage it is written as, "All things are lawful, but not all are helpful. All things are lawful, but not all things build up" (I Corinthians 10:23). This passage represents the function of the subconscious. The subconscious receives each message as though it were law. Some of these messages are strong and positive. As a result the subconscious law which we are compelled to obey leads us to a full and happy life. Unfortunately some messages tear down the self-image, and those too are accepted as law. Be careful what you are sending: it is all accepted as the law.

Whether you gain or lose points is the option of your conscious mind. If you handle a situation in a manner consistent with your belief system, your conscious will deem that you have done something of quality, and will send a positive message to your subconscious. This will improve your self-image. You must be faithful to your basic values and beliefs, whatever they may be, in order to gain points. Make sure you are continually sending messages that direct your self-image in the direction you want to go.

Your *basic beliefs* are a part of your self-image. They are a result of previous teachings, heredity, customs, and all other messages or points already stored in your subconscious. Many of these message were provided you as a result of your heritage and were determined prior to your birth. Some of your beliefs no longer apply or are now destructive. These too must be overcome through replacement messages. Therefore, as you change your self-image, you change your basic belief system.

If you were raised in poverty, you may have a fundamental belief that you are meant to be poor. This is nonsense! You must make a conscious effort to change this belief by sending prosperity messages to your subconscious. In this manner you will change your nature and will achieve financial success in direct proportion to the strength of your new beliefs that you deserve it.

These rules apply to all forms of limiting beliefs. You are not condemned to ill-health, loneliness, drudgery, or fear any more than you are to being poor. The choice is yours to make if you are willing to make the effort to gain enough points to overcome your self-imposed limitations.

Gaining and Losing Points

Unlike all men, all points are not created equal. Of course the subconscious records all points with equal alacrity. It is the conscious which determines the value of the points sent. There are seven components to your self-image points. Each of these components has some control over the point value and thereby the resultant impact on your self-image.

1. *Intensity.* The intensity of emotion behind your message dictates the impact the message will have on your subconscious and thereby the number of points tallied. Repeat the same mundane affirmation over and over with little or no feeling, and you will not budge your self-image very far. Instead, send a message with intensity, and your subconscious will take notice immediately.

2. *Frequency.* The more often your subconscious receives a message, the more it will count it. If you tell yourself you are a winner on a daily basis, you will soon believe it. In a later chapter we talk about affirmations and their impact on our self-image. Be cautious however. One very intense damnation can negate a thousand unemotional positive messages.

3. *Clarity.* The clearer the message, the easier it is for your subconscious to classify and record it. The subconscious does not function well with mixed messages. It will try to make sense of them within the framework of the existing self-image, potentially turning a gain into a loss. Therefore be clear in your conscious mind about the outcome of all your actions. Learn to think clearly and precisely. You will then send the message to your subconscious as you intend it.

4. *Consistency.* The subconscious mind will record points in a manner consistent with your existing self-image and belief system. If you rob a convenience store and try to convince yourself that it was a good and nurturing endeavor, your subconscious probably will not increase your score. Instead it will reduce your tally because robbery is an activity contrary to your beliefs in right and wrong.

5. *Sensory Involvement.* The greater the number of senses involved in an event, the greater the points. See, hear, feel, smell, and taste victory. Relish life with all your being and you will rapidly accumulate points.

6. *Impact.* The greater the pain or pleasure you associate with an event, the greater the point score will be. If there is intense pleasure derived from your actions, you will gain points. Experience intense pain, and you will lose.

Beware of conflicts with your belief system. If you enjoy short-term pleasure at the price of long-term pain, you will lose points. The pleasure of gluttony is not enough to compensate for the greater pain which will surely follow.

7. *Magnitude.* The more dramatic an action, the greater the point value. If you find a wallet in the street and anonymously return it, you gain mega-points. You are telling your subconscious that you are honest and caring beyond reproach. Do great acts in a noble way, and you will increase your self-esteem very rapidly.

Practice Makes Perfect

The self-image can be likened to a muscle. It is not possible to build up a muscle overnight. It requires a great deal of work to strengthen it.

If you have a negative self-image, you usually react negatively unless you make a conscious effort to do otherwise. Therein lies your greatest asset. You can change your mind to change your life. With a modicum of effort you can choose to take the positive path in a given situation thereby adding to your point total. As you accumulate points, it becomes even easier to accumulate more.

What Is Your Score?

How can you tell what your point score is? Evaluate your life. Take an inventory of your assets and liabilities. Look at your accomplishments, near-misses, and failures. If you are really bold, ask others for their evaluation of your life.

The next chapter identifies characteristics of those with low self-esteem and enumerates several ways in which point losses occur. Chapter 4 identifies those traits associated with high self-esteem winners and identifies several means to gain points. See how you relate to the descriptions provided in both chapters and then determine which behavior most closely parallels your own. If you are honest, you will see a direct correlation between your past actions and the results you are experiencing today.

CHAPTER SUMMARY

1. There are no neutral events. Your every thought and action creates an opportunity for you to acquire self-esteem points.

2. The conscious mind edits your actions and sends messages to your subconscious consistent with your belief system. In other words, your conscious mind determines whether your subconscious receives positive or negative messages.

3. Your subconscious does not know if a message is positive or negative. It merely stores the messages and then tallies all messages in its own scoring system. Therefore a positive message sent from the conscious will offset a negative message already in the subconscious. Of course, a negative message will also offset an existing positive message.

4. Your self-image is based upon the sum of all of the messages stored in the subconscious. Your subconscious will direct you to actions consistent with the self-image it holds for you. This self-image is derived from a lifetime of gaining and losing points.

5. The more points you have accumulated, the more likely your subconscious is to impel you to succeed. These points will not change the cards you are dealt but will improve the way that you play them. Winners find a way to win, losers find a way to lose.

6. The number of points associated with a thought or act is dictated by your emotional intensity, its frequency, the clarity with which your subconscious receives the message, its consistency with your belief system, the number of senses with which you have the experience, the pain or pleasure associated with the action, and its magnitude.

7. As you earn points it will be easier to acquire even more. Your subconscious will impel you to succeed, which in turn enables the conscious to send more positive messages to the subconscious. This is a form of compound interest on compound interest.

3

Losing Points

L IFE IS A BURDEN FOR THOSE WITH A TERRIBLE SELF-IMAGE. Their best days are uncomfortable, their worst unbearable. Instead of relishing life and viewing it as a gift, they curse their situation and crave escape. Unless they consciously re-program their subconscious mind, they cannot escape the consequences of their lack of self-esteem.

"You cannot do wrong without suffering wrong" (Emerson, "Compensation"). Those who do wrong lose points and those who lose too many points suffer—forfeiting even more points for their misery.

The loser is propelled to destruction by his own subconscious mind. It forces him to play the role of a failure whose actions produce an even greater point deficit. Unless the cycle is broken, the loser continues to decline in a spiral of ever-diminishing self-esteem.

The following list identifies the consequences of a negative self-image:

- A lack of success in any endeavor.

- General unhappiness.

- Nervousness manifested by tics, foot tapping, nail biting, fidgeting, and lack of eye contact.

- Vacuousness characterized by being:
  - absentminded
  - accident prone
  - forgetful
  - indecisive
  - prone to losing things.

- Demonstrating unhealthy behavior of:
  - arrogance
  - boasting
  - complaining
  - escapism through television, radio, music, reading, or sleeping
  - excessive daydreaming
  - lack of commitment
  - lying
  - messiness
  - over-talking
  - poor eating habits
  - poor grooming
  - procrastination
  - rationalization
  - rudeness
  - sloppiness in work
  - slovenly appearance
  - smoking
  - tardiness.

- Mindlessly subscribing to the latest fad diet, exercise program, clothes style, or self-help program.

- Continually experiencing financial difficulty.

- Suffering poor health induced by hypochondria or psychosomatic illness.

- Experiencing insecurity, unfounded fear, and phobias.

- Demonstrating neuroses or paranoia.

- Exhibiting anti-social behavior including excessive speeding, dishonesty, prejudice, bigotry, theft, excessive anger, and resentments.

- Indulging in obsessive behavior through drunkenness, over-eating, over-working, drug abuse, gambling, excessive spending, or a preoccupation with sex.

- Depression.

- Entering into and remaining in abusive relationships.

- Practicing self-destructive behavior such as bulimia, anorexia nervosa, and self-immolation.

- Homicide.

- Suicide.

It is impossible to disguise a negative self-image; it will always manifest in some form of undesirable behavior. Observe those who profess to be secure, confident, and successful. Do they look you in the eye when they talk? Do they smoke two packs of cigarettes a day? Are they constantly fidgeting or chattering like a magpie? Perhaps they are not as self-assured as they wish you to believe.

Are you trying to cover a deficit by pretending all is well? You cannot do it for long; eventually your behavior will betray you. Examine your life to determine which of the negative characteristics described above you demonstrate. Be honest when evaluating the quality of your life. Are you happy? Do you have secure, loving relationships? Are you successful?

If you are not satisfied with your life, you are not alone. Thoreau (1854) wrote, "The mass of men lead lives of quiet desperation." If you are one of them, if you suffer a negative self-image in any area of your life, make an effort to stop losing points and compensate for the deficit you already have.

Loss of Points

How do you lose self-esteem points? You do it simply by behaving in a way that is contrary to your conscience. Conscience is defined as "the knowledge of one's own thoughts and actions as right or wrong; the moral faculty of distinguishing right from wrong; sense of right and wrong" (Webster's Dictionary). When you act in a manner that your conscience knows to be wrong, you lose points. In short, when you act like a loser, you become one.

Right and wrong are very subjective states. What one may view as proper, another will condemn as corrupt. For instance, in some Eskimo and South Pacific societies it is considered mannerly for a husband to submit his wife to sleep with an overnight guest. It is bad form for the visitor to refuse such an invitation. The tribal member, his wife, and the guest all lose points if the offer is refused. In Western cultures this practice would be viewed as immoral, and all those who participated would strain their conscience. Be true to your personal beliefs; it is the only sure way to avoid losing points.

Your opinion of the quality of your life best indicates whether you have a balance or a shortage of self-esteem points.

If you are true to your conscience you will be the first to know it. Epicurus (c. 290 BC) wrote, "It is not possible to live pleasantly without living prudently and honorably and justly, nor again to live a life of prudence, honor, and justice without living pleasantly." Are you living pleasantly? If not, you have a point deficit, most likely as the result of one or more of the following causes:

Conditions at birth. If it is true that all men are created equal, then the circumstances surrounding conception and birth certainly separate them. Some are born into poverty and misery, abuse, physical impairment, or hatred. Immediately the subconscious is bombarded with negative messages. Even the collective consciousness of race and nationality can imprint negativity upon a child's self-image; many have inherited several generations worth. The sins of the fathers and their fathers before them are truly visited upon the children.

Some babies are born addicted to drugs, while others are deformed from the drug and alcohol abuse of their mothers. Many people chemically alter their genes by ingesting mind-altering substances, then irresponsibly beget children cursed with birth defects.

These disadvantages are indeed heartbreaking and certainly not the fault of the child. Fortunately no one is condemned to continue any inherited negative patterns. It is possible to alter one's apparent destiny through the accumulation of enough self-esteem points.

If you were born with any of these disadvantages, it will be of no value to deny their existence, nor to angrily denounce them. Accept your heritage or you will only lose more points. You must first acknowledge who you are before you can change. All roads may lead to Rome, but you must know on which you are traveling before you can move in the right direction.

The next three chapters are devoted to demonstrating ways to add points to your self-image, as well as methods to recover from the losses you already have suffered. Practice these techniques, and you will be able to overcome any inherited handicap —physical, mental, emotional, or spiritual. Study the remaining descriptions to see where you lose points. Correct your negative behavior, and you will improve the quality of your life. Those of you suffering low self-esteem, due to heredity or any other reason, will be able to stop your slide into the abyss of despair.

Messages from parents, relatives, friends, teachers, and associates. Hugh Prather wrote, "It's obvious that many of the problems I have are the result of how things were when I was growing up. So here I am spending the rest of my life suffering for personality traits I never asked for. Where is the justice in that? There isn't any. But I was never promised justice" (Prather, 1977).

During childhood you probably accepted everything told you by authority figures. You were mostly defenseless against these pronouncements—be they complimentary or derogatory. If all you heard were a slew of insults, you no doubt developed a poor self-image.

As you matured, you learned to edit the comments of others. Still, if you now have a poor self-image and continue to receive negative messages, your conscious mind automatically accepts them. It is even more insidious when you are bestowed a compliment. In those instances, the message is inconsistent with your self-image and you actually reverse it. You turn sincere praise into a loss of points by consciously disagreeing.

You can overcome any negative personality traits you may have acquired as a child. One way is to practice turning all external messages positive before sending them to your subconscious. Accept compliments graciously and fight the urge to question their sincerity. Stop automatically accepting insults and constructive criticism; instead, reverse such negativity by turning them into positive statements (see Chapter 5 for affirmation techniques).

The Inner Voice. There is a part of your mind that is always chattering at you. It doesn't stop even when you sleep. This creature is constantly sending messages to your subconscious by placing a value on everything. You may see a luxury car and think, "It would be nice if I could have a car like that." But, your inner voice will counter with, "You'll never be able to afford it." Catch yourself when you hear this internal voice saying a negative comment. Counter with a positive affirmation, better yet, counter with several.

Negative Self-talk. Self-talk is a more conscious form of self-generated messages than is the inner voice. You may catch yourself saying, "You are sure dumb. Why did you say that anyhow?" If you spoke to your friends this same way, you would soon be very lonely. When you conduct negative self-talk, you speak directly to your subconscious and your point deficit grows rapidly. Be aware of this trait. Make a conscious effort to control it by reversing the self-talk from negative to positive. You will eliminate a great deal of unnecessary pain and will become a friend to yourself.

Imagining the worst. Your subconscious is not aware of the original source of any messages it receives. An event can occur entirely within your mind or may actually transpire—it matters not to your subconscious. Beware then of imagining negative outcomes and of creating problems where none exist. Here is a tale to illustrate:

A salesman was driving a rental car down a country road, passing several farms on his way. It was late and he was anxious to get to the next town and his hotel. Suddenly he lost control when the car swerved toward the side of the road. He braked to a stop and was relieved to find it was only a flat tire.

"No problem," he told himself. "These rentals are always well-equipped for something like this. I'll be on my way in no time." Much to his disappointment, he discovered that while the trunk held a spare tire, it lacked a jack.

"No problem," he told himself. "I'll just walk back to that last farmhouse. It's only a short way and the farmer will surely have a jack I can borrow. In fact, I'll bet he'll drive me back here and change the tire for me. These people are so nice."

As he walked, he imagined the farmer resting comfortably in his house. "He may not want to help me," argued the salesman to himself. "After all I am a stranger and these people are awfully closed-minded around here."

"No problem," he told himself. "After all, what kind of a salesman would I be if I couldn't talk one of these yokels out of a lousy jack."

He continued to walk and continued to think. In his mind, he first saw the farmer as a kindly man, then as a recluse, and finally as an ogre who hoarded his possessions and feared strangers.

"Maybe it won't be a problem if I beg the s.o.b. and offer him money," the salesman coached himself. "I sure do need that jack so I can get out of this lousy place."

The further he walked the more agitated he became. Finally he reached the front door of the farmhouse where he rapped loudly. A kindly gentleman answered the door promptly, looked at the now disheveled salesman, and asked, "May I help you?"

"I wouldn't take your damn jack even if you gave it to me!" shouted the salesman to the bewildered farmer. With that he stormed back to his car where he spent the night sitting in the front seat staring at the sky and cursing his misfortune.

This old story demonstrates how you can lose points entirely through your imagination. The salesman had no empirical evidence that he would be refused, yet he agitated himself into a state of rage.

Take care the next time you find yourself playing a game of "He'll say this, then I'll say that, then he'll say this. . . ." You are creating a loss of points entirely within your own mind. Practice instead visualizing positive outcomes. It takes the same amount of energy, is more pleasant, and results in a gain of points instead of a loss.

Daydreaming. We all daydream. Indulging in the fantasy of living on a tropical island surrounded by natural beauty can be a very pleasant escape. When you daydream a life that makes your own seem inadequate, you lose points. James Thurber created a character named Walter Mitty ("The Secret Life of Walter Mitty") who typified this condition. Though his own life was dull, Walter Mitty indulged in daydreams where he was always the hero. It helped him cope with his own dull and hen-pecked existence, but did nothing to improve the quality of his life.

When you indulge in such fantasy, it may help you contend with an unhappy situation. Unfortunately such an exercise is quite harmful. You always feel worse upon returning from your reverie. You lose points by telling your subconscious that your life is dull and uninteresting, and you are incapable of improving it.

Use daydreaming to gain points. Imagine yourself reaching practical goals and achieving success. You can still be a hero, just be realistic about it. Later in this book you will learn visualization techniques you can use for your daydreams as well.

Practicing the seven deadly sins. Pride, greed, lust, anger, gluttony, envy, and sloth are not sins against God, nature, or your fellow beings. Instead, they are sins against yourself. Each of the seven deadly sins describes behavior that is an abuse of your natural instincts. Emmet Fox said, "The soul's integrity is the one and only thing that matters" (Fox, 1938). By indulging in any of these practices you are losing points and causing yourself harm; you are violating your soul's integrity. Don't sell your dignity and honor for the price of any of these indulgences.

> *Pride.* "Pride goes before destruction, and a haughty spirit before a fall" (Proverbs 16:18). It is normal to enjoy your accomplishments and to strive for perfection. It is not healthy to seek constant recognition or to place insensitive demands on yourself or others in the name of pride. Your pride will eventually destroy you. Prior to that, it will detract from your every triumph. Do your best because you want to, not because of a compelling need to maintain a prideful facade.

Greed. Greed is an extreme form of the desire for security. When you are greedy, you are really telling yourself that you are incapable of handling your affairs, that you must hoard your material goods, not for pleasure, but from fear. Greed reduces the joy of having and of being; it expresses a lack of confidence. Be prudent. Save your money, provide for your security, and enjoy your possessions. Avoid selfish motivations; they cost you points.

Lust. Lust is a loss of control. You lose points through the undignified and foolish acts you commit seeking an outlet for your carnal cravings. Express love and enjoy sex, but avoid unhealthy encounters. Channel your thoughts away from lust and into something more productive.

Anger. Anger is also a loss of control and is born of frustration and a lack of love. You are adversely stimulated by people or circumstances. You lose control of your feelings and your life by reacting negatively to these outside influences.

Once you are already angry, acknowledge it. You lose points by denying your feelings or by making them wrong. Accept your anger but control it by avoiding irrational acts. As you gain enough points to love yourself and to accept others, your anger will dissipate.

Gluttony. Any time you overindulge in food or drink to a level of discomfort you detract from your self-image. You not only jeopardize your physical well-being, you also tell your subconscious you are unable to control your appetites or even act sensibly.

Envy.   Winners cheer for others; losers envy. When you envy others, you lose points by placing yourself beneath them. Understand that any blessing available to another can be yours as well. Cheer for others' good fortune, for it proves that success is possible.

Sloth.   Sloth is another way of saying lazy. Laziness indicates a fear of life. When you avoid your duties and responsibilities, you lose points. You often compound the loss by adding guilt for your failure to act.

You can be very subtle in your practice of sloth. Francis Bacon (1625) wrote, "To spend too much time in studies is sloth." Don't over-plan your actions or you will be tired before you begin. Activity is a habit. Acquire it and you will avoid the point loss associated with sloth.

Other negative conduct.   Lying, cheating, stealing, cussing, swearing, even speeding create a loss of points. By practicing such negative behavior you warn your subconscious that you need an edge, that you are incapable of success on your own merits. Practice proper behavior in all circumstances regardless of the results. You will gain enough positive points to offset any external disadvantages you may encounter.

Slovenly behavior.   Tardiness, carelessness, untidiness, poor eating habits, smoking, and a lack of manners are signs of low self-esteem, and perpetuate a point loss unless the cycle is broken. Practice agreeable behavior and soon your self-esteem will be high enough that such actions will be natural. Each time you make your bed, brush your teeth, shower, eat a well-balanced meal, and arrive on time, you gain points. These points accumulate quickly to lead to higher self-esteem. Remember that every event results in either a gain or a loss of points. Take advantage of these simple acts to gain points each day.

Association with negative people. In the poem "Desiderata" (Anonymous) you are advised to "Avoid loud and aggressive persons, they are vexations to the spirit." Negative people complain and assume the roles of victims. When you associate with them, you become one of them. Your self-esteem drops and you lose points. To your subconscious, you are known by the company you keep.

Associate with winners and soon you will become one. Your friends can be your most important asset. Epicurus wrote, "Of all the things which wisdom acquires to produce the blessedness of the complete life, far the greatest is the possession of friendship." Do you have enough wisdom to acquire and cherish nurturing, supportive friendships?

Sex with people you don't respect. When you have sex with someone you don't respect, you are generating messages that you do not value your capacity to love, nor do you have much self-respect. Prove your self-worth by avoiding promiscuous behavior. When you have accumulated enough love and self-respect points, you will naturally attract someone worthy of your affection.

Failure breeds more failure. The habit of losing is insidious. When you fail, you lose points. This lowers your self-image, which then makes it easier to fail again, costing you even more points. Break the cycle. Practice winning by setting easily achievable goals, then attaining them. Each success is worth points. Gradually increase your challenges, and you will gradually increase your point score. The resultant improvement to your self-image will make you a winner.

Poor selection for a career. You lose points every day of your life if you dislike your job or your career. It is difficult to get up in the morning, your self-image suffers, time drags, and the quality of your work cannot possibly be very high. You even suffer during weekends and holidays because the prospect of returning to work looms in the recesses of your mind.

It is better to find work you enjoy. No amount of money or prestige can compensate you for the loss of self-esteem that you suffer from poor selection of a career. Conversely, performing work you enjoy will allow you to gain points which may well drive you to great success.

Rationalization. Rationalization is the process of excusing your behavior, often through use of faulty logic. It is actually a form of lying. When you rationalize your behavior, you send mixed messages to your subconscious. You create confusion by seeming to endorse actions that are contrary to your basic beliefs. As a result, you lose more points than if you had just acknowledged your negative behavior and accepted the consequences.

Have enough self-respect to tell yourself the truth. You really cannot successfully lie to yourself anyhow, and your attempts only create confusion within your subconscious. Such disorientation causes you to be tentative and indecisive. Your behavior betrays your dishonesty.

Comparison. "Desiderata" advises, "If you compare yourself with others, you may become vain and bitter; for always there will be greater and lesser persons than yourself." When you practice comparison, you are effectively ranking yourself among others. Whether you place them above or beneath you, you lose points. Learn to accept yourself for who you are and you will be able to accept others. Work on increasing your points to improve your self-image, and understand that others are blessed or limited by their own point total.

Judgment.   There are a number of ways your judgment causes you to lose points. One of the most perverse results is that it causes loneliness. When you judge someone or something, you are defining that entity as something separate and different from yourself. Each judgment has the effect of setting you slightly apart from the rest of the world. As you increase your judgments, you widen the gap between yourself and others. Soon you feel forlorn, unique, and misunderstood. You come to fear attack, and eventually develop paranoia and practice isolation. You slink through life in the shadows trying not to be noticed.

Reduce your judgments and you narrow your separation. Find similarities instead of differences and learn to accept others. They have a great deal to teach you—if only you can look past your judgment.

Prejudice and bias.   Prejudice and bias are also forms of judgment as well as forms of fear. Whenever you condemn a race, creed, sex, or ethnic group, you are expressing a fear to your subconscious. You are telling it that there is an entire group of people who are so different from you that they are a threat. You must protect yourself against them. This causes you to retreat into the shadows of life because your subconscious believes there are enemies everywhere.

We are all prejudiced because we are all fearful. Admit your prejudices and practice reducing them. Learn something about those you hate. With your knowledge will come an understand-

ing which will reduce your prejudice and your fear. Remember
that many people are born with a point deficit. You want
understanding for your lack of points, so understand theirs.

Gossip, character assassination, and revenge.   Each of these acts is a
form of murder. Speak unkindly toward a person, attack his
character, or exact retribution for a perceived wrong, and you
destroy a part of him. This causes you a great deal of harm. You
certainly acquire guilt and probably feel remorse. Even if you
justify your actions, you still admit to a certain lack of class.
George Eliot (1874) wrote, "Gossip is a sort of smoke that comes
from the dirty tobacco-pipes of those who diffuse it; it proves
nothing but the bad taste of the smoker."
      Forgive your enemies and they lose all power over you.
Continue to plot against them and you provide them free rent
in the forefront of your mind. When you think about it, resentments are silly. You are punishing yourself in the present for
something someone else did to you in the past. Rise above such
pettiness and you will grow free of resentments and find a
renewed energy for more positive activities.

Avoidance of difficult situations.   You demonstrate a fear of life
when you avoid its unpleasantries. They occur regularly and only
compound when you resist them. Any difficult situation you
shirk is still there; you cannot make it disappear by ignoring it.
Instead, it acquires a greater and greater power over you, and
you dread it even more. You lose self-esteem points through your
fearful evasions, and you reduce your ability to perform in the
future.
      Learn to handle each issue as soon as it arises. Avoid
procrastination. Each time you act swiftly and decisively you
gain points, regardless of the outcome. As you acquire more

points, you will find it easier to face unpleasant situations. Soon you will automatically handle difficulties.

Escapism. You lose points whenever you avoid life through reading, sleeping, watching television, or any number of other outlets. Of course you need to relax and renew your spirit. It is only when you use such diversions to ignore your responsibilities that you pay a price.

Develop a balanced life between duty, work, and recreation, but take care of your responsibilities first. You will enjoy your amusements more if you do not have any lingering obligations preying on your mind.

Passive/aggressive behavior. Passive/aggressive behavior is also caused by fear. You are afraid to assert yourself and so acquiesce. This causes you to first lose points due to your cowardice, then compound your losses through destructive behavior. You may meekly accept a work assignment with which you disagree, but sabotage the results to gain revenge. All you are really doing is compounding your own negative self-image.

If you oppose someone's point of view but aren't assertive enough to state your own, at least keep any agreements you promised—even if they were made under duress. As you develop self-confidence through the accumulation of points, you will find it easier to express yourself and stand by your beliefs.

Expectation. When you place expectations upon yourself, an event, or another person, you are pre-judging the outcome. Often you are disappointed. That causes a loss of points because you were wrong and soon believe that you cannot rely on anything.

Epictetus (c. 60 AD) wrote, "Ask not that events should happen as you will, but let your will be that events should happen as they do, and you will have peace."

Do your best in all your affairs and avoid placing any expectations on the results. You will be able to eliminate the point loss of disappointment.

Exaggeration. When you exaggerate, you attempt to create an image of yourself and your world that is larger than the truth. Your actual self-image must pale in comparison. Even if the quality of your life is good and your accomplishments outstanding, they will look puny when compared with your fabricated portrayal. Exaggeration costs points because it makes you feel below standard and leads you to believe no one would ever care for the real you. These feelings of inadequacy compel you to exaggerate even more, generating a still greater point loss. Eventually you feel like a phony even when you accomplish something of merit.

Beware of embellishing on your past accomplishments. These stories of your exploits may seem like money in the bank—they gain interest over the years, but they are harmful in two ways. First, they make your present lifestyle seem empty by comparison, and second, they cause you to live in the past and not function in the present.

Tell the truth about yourself and you will be amazed at the reactions. People will readily accept you and feel closer to you, for you will seem more human and approachable. Those you are trying so hard to impress can probably make a fairly accurate assessment of your character anyhow, so lying gains you nothing.

Improve the negative self-image which originally compelled you to exaggerate, and you will come to love yourself for who you are. You will most certainly discover that you are really quite a special person.

Superstition. Superstition is the act of correlating events that have no apparent connection. It is unhealthy and causes you to lose points. If you wear the same shirt for every golf tournament, you are abrogating any power you have to an old piece of cloth. When you are superstitious, you reduce your responsibility and control over a situation. Even if you win, you still lose points by attributing a portion of the victory to some absurd outside influence.

Learn to trust yourself and to value your talents. They are surely more powerful than any talisman.

Over indulgence in food, alcohol, drugs, sex, work, or spending. Sensual pleasures carried to an extreme become obsessive behavior. For many it is an enjoyable activity to indulge in a scrumptious feast and a glass of wine. You lose points, however, when you fail to heed Ben Franklin's (1758) advice to, "Eat not to dullness, drink not to elevation."

The same advice applies to excessive shopping, promiscuity, work, or any other obsessive-compulsive activity. You rapidly lose points when you indulge in any activity after it has ceased to be a pleasure.

Enjoy life and the pleasures it has to offer. Learn to leave something for the next time; it will help you avoid the ill-effects of over-consumption.

Fear. The experience of fear actually reinforces the negative, and encourages your subconscious to seek the very situation you wish to avoid. It is written in Job 3:25: "For the thing that I fear comes upon me and what I dread befalls me." When we fear, we send high-energy negative messages to the subconscious. Negative messages charged with strong emotion imprint the subconscious with greater influence than do those with little emphasis. Remember that the subconscious does not edit messages to determine if they are healthy or damaging. When it receives one of these strong fear-based messages, it forces you to act in a compulsively destructive manner. It is incapable of doing otherwise.

Do not dwell on your fears or you will only increase their likelihood of occurring. Instead deal with them in a positive manner through the visualization and desensitization techniques described in Chapter 5.

Guilt. While guilt is a point-depleting activity, it is actually close to being something quite positive. Guilt may be non-productive, but does suggest a willingness to accept responsibility—which is a very point-enriching endeavor. There are two negative aspects of guilt. You either take responsibility for more than you can control, or you use it as an excuse to continue negative behavior. You accept too much responsibility when you feel guilty for someone else's sadness. You lie to yourself when you pretend to feel guilty for over-eating, yet don't stop doing it. Learn to accept the ways of others and of the world while taking responsibility for your own behavior. Forgive yourself for past indiscretions while learning from them. Resolve to improve while releasing the burden of past mistakes. Guilt will slip away.

Creating chaos. It is possible to become addicted to adrenalin, which is a stimulating rush equal to that of many drugs. Beware of this addiction! You may find yourself creating chaos just to satisfy your urges for a fix. If you doubt whether you are susceptible to this malady, check your reactions while watching a well-contested sports event, a fight, or the dramatic confrontations of a television drama. Are you stimulated? If so, you understand the feeling.

Evaluate your behavior to determine where you are similarly aroused through your own activities. Do you compound issues and force confrontations just to feel a high? Do you relish living on the edge? Are your relationships stormy? Do you try to juggle too many balls at the same time? Answer yes, and you are probably addicted to your own adrenalin.

A healthy exuberance and passion for life is necessary to be a winner. It is when you channel that energy into chaotic turmoil that you pay a price in point loss and lowered self-esteem. Practice relaxation techniques; substitute positive challenges for negative ones; reduce artificial arousal by avoiding television action programs and sports events; and improve your diet by eliminating spicy foods, caffeine, and sugar.

There is a natural high associated with living a quality life which is far superior to a frenzied adrenalin high. Chaos costs points. You can gain them back by leading an orderly life.

Hypocrisy. Beware of taking action merely to maintain a facade. When you perform to gain credit, or to impress others, you are lying. You lose more points for your insincerity than you gain through your deeds. It is better to withhold charity than to give begrudgingly for social recognition. Don't feign honor in public and practice deceit in private; it is of no value. Gain enough points to love yourself, and soon you will naturally act honorably and properly because you enjoy it. There is a great deal of pleasure to be had in helping others because you want to.

Accepting the role of victim. When you accept the role of victim, you send a message to your subconscious that there is someone or something with the purpose and power to ruin your life. You abrogate your accountability. Learn to take responsibility for your actions and you will actually gain positive points from negative outcomes.

There are many vehicles you can ride when you assume the role of victim. You may take advice from someone, then blame them when the outcome is unsatisfactory. You can rationalize that others did not put out their best effort and therefore you became a victim of circumstances beyond your control. You can alibi your behavior rather than take action to correct it. Here is a sampler of a victim's alibis:

- I can't because I don't have the education.

- I can't because I have poor health.

- If only I were born in a better neighborhood.

- I wish I were taller, smarter, or more outgoing.

- If only I were married.

- If only I were single and didn't have these kids.

- I never get any breaks, I have such terrible luck.

Never allow yourself to wear the cloak of a victim, no matter what the circumstances. You always lose points when you do. Instead, determine your responsibility in all unpleasantries and resolve to improve. Remember that you have a choice for every path you take. If you have an undesirable mate, consider your decisions which led to the union in the first place, as well as your culpability for any current difficulties. If you have a poor job, either quit or quit complaining. Slavery was long ago abolished and there are no more indentured servants. If you lack education, go to school. Do something! You always have some responsibility for every situation in your life. You always have the ability to change.

Heed the words of John Dewey in *Morals and Conduct*: "What others do to us when we act is as natural a consequence of our action as what the fire does to us when we plunge our hands in it." Others do not do it to you, you do it to yourself. Remember this always.

How do you play the role of victim? What are your alibis? Stop being a victim and you will soon view your life from the entirely new perspective of a winner.

All of these actions cost points. How many of them do you practice? Your level of development is directly attributable to your own behavior. Be aware of all the ways you lose points and work to break out of the cycle.

Every event in your life results in a gain or a loss of points. As you build a surplus you will notice it becomes easier to function in a healthy manner. Negative behavior generates more of the same, while positive activity increases self-esteem and an ability to succeed. If you have money in the bank, it grows from the dividends you earn; if you owe, your debt grows from the service charges you are assessed. Compound interest on compound interest works both ways. The rich get richer, the poor get poorer; winners win, losers lose. Once you cross the line to a balance of points, you become a winner. You are on the road to riches in all aspects of your life.

CHAPTER SUMMARY

1. It is impossible to completely hide a poor self-image. The greater point deficit one has, the worse the consequences. Low self-esteem manifests in many forms, from nervousness and a lack of success to the extreme of suicide.

2. Be true to your conscience. It is your best guide to proper behavior.

3. Evaluate your behavior to determine what you do to cost yourself points. Correct your behavior, and your life will improve. Guaranteed!

4. As you gain points, it will be easier to acquire even more.
   Your subconscious will impel you to succeed, which in turn
   will enable the conscious to generate more positive messages. This is a form of compound interest on compound
   interest.

4

Gaining Points

OH HOW DELIGHTFUL IS LIFE for those with a positive self-image. Each day is an adventure to the people who possess enough confidence to face any situation. They savor every opportunity to use their gifts and talents, and to experience all that life has to offer. These winners leap from their beds to face the morning, live a full and active day, then begrudgingly retire at night. They don't find it necessary to escape into the oblivion of a bottle, pill, or powder; nor do they need to overeat, fantasize, or distract themselves with endless hours of television. They face life head on and are glad to be alive. The only requirement you must fulfill to enjoy a winner's life is to accumulate an abundance of self-esteem points. If you identified with the behavior discussed in the last chapter, you may be saying that it is fine to learn ways to lose points; you are already well-practiced at it. What you really need to know is how you can amass a fortune in positive points and enjoy the benefits of a healthy self-image. Read on and see how easy it can be for you to enjoy the good life.

Cultivate A Winner's Attitude

Your attitude is the key to your success. Those who face life head on and relish the challenge are continually acquiring points. They enjoy life and view it as an adventure. To them life is a feast to be enjoyed, not a drudge to be endured. Observe how winners enjoy a challenge. They volunteer to speak at the convention; they take responsibility for the project; they shoot the ball with three seconds left and the game on the line. They take these actions because they have a winner's outlook and the entire store of points that such optimism brings. You too can become a winner by first developing a winner's attitude.

Without a doubt your attitude determines more point values than does any other characteristic with which you are endowed. Once again, remember that your subconscious does not edit the messages it receives, but merely accumulates them in the structure called your self-image. Before any messages are sent to your subconscious, they are edited by your conscious mind, where values are placed on the data.

If you have a well-developed positive mental attitude, your editor will find a way to create positive self-esteem points from any event or thought. Edison was unsuccessful in his first thousand attempts to perfect the light bulb. He was asked if he was at all discouraged.

"Not at all," he replied. "I know that with each failure I am one step closer to success."

This was indeed a man with a positive mental attitude which endowed him with the ability to generate positive self-esteem points from a series of apparently negative events. Winners win and losers lose, often as a result of their attitude toward life. A loser may encounter a temporary setback and conclude, "Well, it's all over now. It's too late for me to win this. Let me go on to the next thing."

A winner like Edison will say, "I sure learned from that. Now I am better off than before. Let me continue to pursue this matter now that I am closer to victory."

You can acquire a winner's attitude through passion, practice, and persistence. Put some feeling behind all you do; learn to evaluate every event to find the positive outcome; and develop the habits of speaking positively, acting positively, and thinking positively. View a setback as a learning opportunity which actually brings you closer to your goal. You will gain points and find you have acquired a winner's attitude.

Other Traits of Winners

Practicing each item on the following list of traits and disciplines will provide you with an abundant supply of self-esteem points. Continue their practice and you will come to enjoy the rewards of a healthy self-image. You are a winner when you:

Act responsibly in even the most simple matters. You can prove yourself a winner when you perform even the most common tasks. Don't begrudge your daily chores, but enjoy them and do them with love. You can gain points every day of your life through such an attitude. Here is a list of one hundred easy ways to gain points. After you read it, add another hundred of your own. Remember these lists well. Perform one of these tasks whenever you are melancholy or lethargic; the points you gain will raise your spirits.

1. Act politely

2. Assemble a model plane or ship

3. Attend a lecture

4. Balance your checkbook

5. Bathe the dog

6. Bring flowers to a loved one

7. Brush your teeth

8. Carpool

9. Change the bed linen

10. Clean the closet

11. Clean the cupboards

12. Clean your garage

13. Clean your home

14. Coach a team

15. Comb your hair

16. Cook a meal

17. Dispose of something you no longer use

18. Do something nice without being asked or seeking credit

19. Do your laundry

20. Donate unwanted items to charity

21. Donate your time to charity

22. Dress up

23. Drive courteously

24. Drive the speed limit

25. Eat a good breakfast

26. Eat a well-balanced meal

27. File your taxes

28. Floss your teeth

29. Get up early

30. Go for a walk

31. Go to church

32. Go to the library

33. Grocery shop and use coupons to save money

34. Hang your clothes

35. Have a massage

36. Have your teeth cleaned

37. Include a shy person in your conversation

38. Join a support group

39. Keep a secret

40. Label your electrical circuit breakers

41. Laugh

42. Learn something new

43. Listen carefully to someone

44. Make a chores list

45. Make love

46. Make your bed

47. Memorize a poem

48. Mow the lawn

49. Notice a friend's new hair style or new clothes

50. Organize your cupboards

51. Organize your record, tape, and compact disk collections

52. Paint a picture—even if it is paint-by-the-numbers

53. Pay a compliment

54. Pay off a debt

55. Pay your bills

56. Pick some flowers

57. Plant a garden

58. Plant a tree

59. Play a musical instrument

60. Read a book to improve your mind

61. Recycle bottles, cans and newspapers

62. Refuse drugs or drink

63. Replace the top on the toothpaste tube

64. Return phone calls

65. Rotate your tires

66. Save some money

67. Say "I love you" to someone and mean it

68. Say please and thank you

69. Say you are sorry

70. Scrub the floor

71. Send a birthday, Christmas, Father's Day, or Mother's Day card

72. Send a friendship card

73. Service your car

74. Sew your own clothes

75. Show up on time

76. Shop for the best quality and the best price

77. Smile

78. Sympathize

79. Take a class

80. Take a new route to work

81. Take a relaxing bath

82. Take a vacation

83. Take the long way home

84. Teach a child

85. Teach a friend

86. Telephone a friend

87. Tell the truth

88. Tell a joke

89. Turn off the TV

90. Vacuum the carpet

91. Visit someone in a hospital

92. Volunteer

93. Vote

94. Wash the windows

95. Wash your car

96. Wash your hair

97. Water your indoor plants

98. Work an extra half-hour (but no more—workaholics lose points)

99. Write a letter

100. Write a poem

Exercise. When you exercise, you gain points in a number of ways. You feel better physically, improve your appearance, carry yourself well, and exude confidence. You even release chemicals into the brain called endorphins which stimulate you and improve your attitude. Exercise makes you feel good about yourself, which in turn generates positive messages in your subconscious.

Develop a sensible exercise plan without attempting to over-reach your current level of self-esteem. Instead select activities you can enjoy and will do faithfully. As exercise becomes a habit, you can balance your program with aerobic conditioning, stretching, and skeletal and muscular development.

Eat properly. A proper diet will provide you with the energy to accomplish your goals. It will improve the quality of your sleep while reducing the amount you need. Nutritious meals can help you maintain your appearance in several ways. Your weight will stabilize, your hair will shine, your eyes will be clear, your nerves will be steady, and your disposition will be even.

Eat well-balanced and moderate meals, avoiding fad diets. Don't try to lose weight too rapidly; it will only reappear and bring more with it. Develop healthy ways to nurture yourself, and avoid the solace you may derive from burying your feelings under an avalanche of food. Do not use layers of fat to insulate yourself from life. "One should eat to live, and not live to eat" (Moliere, 1669, *L'Avare*).

Avoid sugar. Avoiding sugar could have been included under eating properly, but it is so important it has a category of its own. Overindulgence in sugar causes mood swings which make it difficult for you to maintain a positive attitude no matter how hard you may try. While sugar often gives a quick charge, it forces the pancreas to release an overdose of insulin to compensate. This actually lowers your energy level and causes you to feel tired and lethargic. When you feel that way, you often send your subconscious negative messages that you are lazy or incompetent.

Sugar also raises the body's weight set point. The set point is an internal mechanism which adjusts your metabolism to maintain your weight level. If you reduce your calorie intake, the set point slows your metabolism to compensate. Soon you are eating half your usual amount and still failing to lose weight. When you tire of that spartan routine and return to your normal diet, you gain more pounds. So cut out sugar, as sugar makes it very difficult to maintain a healthy weight level and a healthy self-image. You gain points each time you refuse dessert or resist the temptation to indulge in a sugary snack. Count how long it has been since your last sugar binge; as the days mount so will your points.

Carry yourself with grace and dignity. Winners stand tall, look others in the eye, and speak clearly and forcefully. Practice good posture, stride rather than walk, and make direct eye contact. Avoid unnecessary confrontation and don't whine when you are inconvenienced. Listen carefully to others instead of merely waiting your turn to speak. State your opinion when asked, but stop burdening others with your views. Be of good cheer.

If you are sad or tired, throw back your shoulders, stand erect, and smile. You will feel better immediately.

Choose your words carefully. Each time you speak you are sending a message to your subconscious. Avoid negativity of any type for it only costs you points; instead speak positively to gain them.

Acknowledge your feelings. Accept your feelings, but don't become a slave to them. Experience your emotions, be they pleasant or unpleasant. Grieve, love, be angry or sad if you must; each is proof you are alive. It is unhealthy to deny your feelings, for they will always find an outlet. Ignore them, and you become distraught and suffer physical ailments.

This does not mean you should indulge yourself by overplaying your role. Be disappointed but don't have tantrums; be sad but don't act suicidal; feel joy but don't become manic; feel love but don't mindlessly adore. Your emotions are a gift; they are the greatest proof you have that you are alive. Enjoy them, experience them, acknowledge them, but don't allow them to be a burden.

Keep your word to yourself and others. You gain points and self-respect when you keep your agreements. You demonstrate value for yourself and others by showing up on time, keeping appointments, saying what you mean, and meaning what you say. Never promise anything you have no intention of delivering. Instead, always do what you say you will.

Complete tasks. It is easy to get sidetracked from completing a task, usually for a very good reason. "When you're up to your ass in alligators, it's hard to remember that you're there to drain the swamp." Problems are always arising which make it difficult to finish a job, but winners find a way to finish what they start, regardless of the problems they encounter. In other words, while the alligators may make it difficult to focus on your assignment, they will go away once you actually drain the swamp. Focus on reaching your objective, rather than on the reasons why you can't. Once you succeed, any difficulties you overcame in the process will only increase the number of points you gain.

Do what you enjoy and enjoy what you do. It is much easier to complete what you begin if you enjoy the task. You will always gain points if you take pleasure in your activities, without becoming obsessive or compulsive about them. Select a career because it is something you want to do and not because it offers status, money or power. You will be rewarded in many more ways than you ever dreamed possible—just for doing something you enjoy and doing it well.

Select a hobby or leisure time activity with the same idea, because you enjoy it and not because you want to impress someone, or because it is the latest fad. Remember, there are points in pleasure.

Practice honesty. By being honest in all of your dealings, you are telling the world and yourself that you are confident. You need not resort to chicanery to survive. Your word is indeed your bond and you are brave. Only cowards resort to lying to avoid the consequences of their actions. Only incompetents cheat to reach their goals. You are neither a coward nor an incompetent. Be honest in all you do and your subconscious will soon get the message.

Forgive. Forgiveness is the act of releasing yourself from bondage. If you are like most people, you believe that forgiveness has something to do with other people. That is not accurate. By forgiving, you release the pain within your own heart, thus granting yourself more freedom and energy. You are no longer adversely affected by the past or present actions of another person. This is a very life-enhancing and point-enhancing endeavor.

How do you forgive? Simply decide to. Once you decide to forgive, you are released. If the negative thoughts of anger and resentment resurface, simply dismiss them as no longer holding power over you. Soon these negative feelings will disappear and you will be free. There is a further discussion on forgiveness in Chapter 6. It is included in the section on writing your autobiography. Please refer to it if you find it difficult to practice forgiveness.

Work hard.   Rudyard Kipling wrote, "So the more we work and the less we talk the better results we shall get" *(The Lesson)*. The points you gain from hard work create these better results. Often the difference between success and failure is a willingness to go the extra mile. Once you work hard to become successful, your point gains will build on themselves and compound quickly. You will happily discover that it requires less strain to be a success than it does to be a failure.

What is the real value of hard work? Your efforts tell your subconscious you are willing to participate in life, that you are a doer and not an observer, and that you are willing to put forth whatever effort it requires to succeed. By acquiring the habit of hard work you establish the mental toughness to achieve your goals. In Matthew 5:41, Christ admonished: "If anyone forces you to go one mile, go with him two miles." Heed this advice. Get in the habit of doing more than you are asked and you will soon have more than you ever expected.

Accept and relish change.   Winners understand that change is a part of growth. You cannot improve your life without modifying some phase of it. That means change. When you resist change, you lose points and make your life uncomfortable. When you embrace change, you gain points, grow, and enjoy the stimulation.

Practice temperance. Overindulgence in anything is harmful. You gain points and feel good when you have the discipline to practice temperance in eating, drinking, sex, spending, and work. Don't use any of these activities as a fix for unhappiness or low self-esteem.

If you are initially unable to control your compulsive behavior, work to gain enough points to provide yourself with the self-esteem to resist your temptations. Failing that, join a support group that can guide you in your efforts. Weight Watchers and Alcoholics Anonymous are excellent organizations to help with eating and drinking problems. There are other similar groups for help with any obsessions you may have.

Ask yourself if you are doing something for pleasure or for compulsion. By all means, enjoy life, but don't detract from your delight by surrendering to any form of gluttony. There are points in pleasure, only pain and disappointment in excess.

Simplify your life. You lose points when your life becomes overwhelming, as it does when you have too much on your plate. Simplify. Reduce the clutter in your environment; cultivate a few close friends, rather than a thousand acquaintances; pay off your debts; limit your material goods; and relax. You gain points by living an orderly life.

Pay attention to your environment. Be aware of your surroundings; it makes you feel more alive and less self-centered than when you are preoccupied with your own wants and needs. Pay attention to nature and enjoy the companionship of others, and your life will flow more smoothly.

Act friendly. You can gain points by being nice. Your outlook upon life improves and you feel better about yourself when you are friendly. People respond favorably to you, making it much easier to achieve your goals. Friendly behavior even causes chemical changes in your body, similar to those resulting from healthy exercise.

Behave properly. Take the correct action even if it is difficult. This means that you must listen to your conscience and act accordingly, even if it would be easier to do something else.

Act decisively. Acquire the habit of arriving at a decision and acting on it immediately. Be decisive and forceful. By doing this you generate points and develop a dynamic and powerful personality.

Postpone gratification. You can gain points by doing nothing. Don't surrender to your desires, but wait for an appropriate time to enjoy them. When you demonstrate self-discipline, you feel strong and in control of your life.

Cultivate an attitude of gratitude. "For to every one who has will more be given, and he will have abundance; but from him who has not, even what he has will be taken away" (Matthew 25:29). Why do the rich get richer? They prosper because they are thankful for that which they have. You gain points each time you experience gratitude. It reaffirms the value of your abundance and compels your subconscious to seek even more such gratification. Love that which you have and you will gain even more. This applies to the physical, mental, spiritual, and material realms of your being.

Advantages of Being A Winner

Initially it may seem impossible to practice all of these steps in your life. The good news is that you don't have to. You need not make all of the changes at once, but instead can gradually compensate for a negative self-image by accumulating points. Try then each day to gain more points than you lose. The more points you acquire, the easier it will be to adhere to the conduct prescribed above.

Why would you even want to inflict such discipline into your life? If you want to be a success and lead a happy life you will want to put forth the effort to gain positive points. Once you realize the benefits of an improved self-image, you will discover that winning is actually easier than losing. It may appear that the initial effort is greater to enforce such discipline on yourself, but the reduced pain and complications more than compensate. The following is a partial list of the benefits you enjoy when you accrue an abundance of points—these are the characteristics of a winner:

- Success comes easily and quickly.

- People are drawn to you.

- You radiate power.

- You are happy most of the time.

- You have a love of life which enables you to enjoy more and more of the abundance available to you.

- You enjoy good mental, physical, and spiritual health.

- You enjoy freedom from the fears that paralyze most people.

- You possess high self-esteem.

- You are more relaxed and have freedom from distress.

- You exhibit an intuitive ability to choose the proper course of action.

- You feel a true sense of security.

- You know inner peace and serenity.

- Your relationships with friends, family, and loved ones are magnificent.

Each of these benefits and more are yours if you improve your self-image through positive self-esteem points.

Take a Risk and Get a Point

Take a risk. Take a hundred risks. Set a goal that in the next one hundred days you will take one hundred risks, whatever you define a risk to be. It may be asking for a raise or asking for a date. It may be simply taking a new route to work with the risk of being late, or it may be trying a new recipe and risking disapproval by your family. There is a great deal of value to this exercise. You open your life to more adventure, you expand your comfort zone, and you demonstrate your courage. It matters not the outcome of the event; it only matters that you are willing to take the chance. Every time you take a risk, congratulate yourself. You are building self-esteem points.

When I first did this exercise, I was amazed at the results. I willingly accepted blind dates, initiated conversations, spoke my real opinion when asked, and generally rose above my usual pattern of existence. One time, I peered over a lady's shoulder as she was filling out an application. I wrote down her name and phone number and called her for a date. She was flattered, but turned me down because she was living with her boyfriend. Instead of feeling devastated because it did not work out, I was elated because I took a chance. I reached beyond myself.

"One Small Step . . ."

Another fine way to build your store of positive points without exposing yourself to failure is to generate mini-victories. Managers of fighters have long known that the way to develop a champion is to have him first fight easy opponents. He builds confidence and accumulates success points. They gradually increase the competition until their fighter is of title caliber.

You can do the same thing. Find an activity at which you can easily succeed. Walk a mile, write a letter, pay extra on a bill, or do the TV Guide crossword. It doesn't matter what you do as long as there is a good chance that you will be able to succeed. Unlike the risks, here the outcome does matter.

Gradually increase your challenges until you note a marked improvement. If you walked a mile, walk a mile and a quarter, then a mile and a half. Soon you will be able to walk two miles and feel confident doing it.

Chart your progress. Perhaps you began by walking a mile and are now able to walk four. That is a remarkable improvement. If you then have a difficult time walking four and a half miles, don't despair. After all, you have gone from one to four. Be happy for your gains.

I have often been involved with the hiring and training of new employees. With each of them, I assign an initial task at which I am certain he or she will succeed. I then gradually increase the challenge while praising the accomplishments. In this manner each of them is able to accumulate work points. At the same time, my life is easier because I develop quality employees on whom I can rely. We all succeed. You can do this for your employees, for your children, and for yourself. Establish the habit of winning by winning. In this way you build, in yourself and others, the winning self-images which come from having a storehouse of points.

Set Goals and Get Points For Doing It

We human beings are essentially goal-oriented. We function better when we have a definite purpose to our lives, and have a road map to direct us toward success. Once we establish goals, our subconscious guides us toward them so long as they are consistent with our self-image. Maxwell Maltz (1960) wrote, "Every living thing has a built-in guidance system or goal-striving device, put there by its Creator to help it achieve its goal." The more specific we are in defining our goals, and the more often we ponder and review them, the more points we gain. The more points we have amassed, the more likely we are to achieve our goals.

You can gain an advantage over a majority of your fellow beings if you set specific goals, visualize yourself reaching them, and commit yourself to their accomplishment. By firmly establishing definite goals in your mind, and by continually emphasizing them, you accumulate the points within your subconscious to insure success.

Goal setting is difficult. The reason so few people have specific goals for their lives is that it takes conscious effort and a degree of discipline. It also appears restricting. When I was younger, I believed I had an infinite capacity to experience life. Why would I want to limit myself by writing goals when I could do it all? The more honest reason was that I was shiftless and lacked the necessary discipline to set, then work, toward specific goals.

In retrospect, I realize that those times I did set goals, I often achieved them. I wanted a new and very expensive bicycle, and, though the likelihood was slim, I earned one. When I was in junior high, I dreamed of playing varsity football when I went to high school. I knew I was much too slow and too small, but still I kept my dream. During the summer between my seventh and eighth grade years something marvelous happened: I gained almost forty pounds, grew several inches, and became the fastest runner in my class. I made the team each of my years in high school. Genetics? Perhaps, although no one else in my family was noted for their size or speed. Coincidence? Prescience? There are hundreds of explanations why I was able to realize my aspiration, but I prefer to think the goal setting and visualization had a great deal to do with it.

Intelligent goal setting also contributes to building a positive self-image. Merely having a clear written plan for your life gains points for yourself. Each time you read your goals and picture their achievement in your mind, you accumulate even more points. Once again, if you have fixed goals, your subconscious will guide you toward them so long as they are consistent with your self-image. The more you concentrate on these goals the more points you will accumulate. Achieving your goals is easy once you believe you are worthy.

Perhaps the most difficult aspect of goal setting is finding the goals that are important to you. Few people have fixed goals for their life. They are only aware that they are not happy or successful. Unless you have goals, you will never know if you are successful. It is almost impossible to reach somewhere if you do not know where it is you are going. How would you even know that you have arrived?

Here are some hints to guide you in establishing fixed goals for your life:

1. Make a list of your accomplishments. Write of your victories and moments of glory; remember those special times when all your efforts resulted in success. Write of graduation, marriage, and your first job; describe your promotions and your pleasures in a job well done; list everything you have done of which you are proud.

2. Analyze the list. Place a star beside those items you planned or mentally practiced before you did them. Have you ever rehearsed a job interview in your mind before you actually went to it? Did you often dream of being married long before it ever took place? Did you ever list a goal, then accomplish it? You will probably discover that each of your significant accomplishments was somehow planned or considered prior to its fruition. You are already practicing some form of goal setting.

Each of us is always thinking of something. The mind functions twenty-four hours a day, seven days a week, every day of the year. What you think about you become. "As a man thinketh in his heart so is he" (Allen, *As a Man Thinketh*). Your subconscious mind accepts your thoughts as messages just as it does your actions, and whatever you think about gets interpreted as goals or desirable behavior. Therefore, if you dwell on fears or losses, you are actually directing your subconscious to bring about these difficulties. The purpose of setting goals and visualizing their accomplishment is to direct the subconscious in a healthy and positive manner; it enables you to replace those random and negative thoughts with specific messages of your choosing.

3. Determine if you are satisfied with your life's accomplishments.
Have you achieved any of your childhood dreams? Your adult
dreams? If you died today, would you have left the world a better
place? Or would the world be a better place because you left?

4. Write a biography of your dreams and aspirations. Write the story
of a winner, and allow your imagination to soar. It is a biography
rather than an autobiography, so it is to be written in the third
person. This way you can wax eloquent about yourself without
needing to feign modesty. Describe your physical, emotional,
and spiritual states; add what you have attained in your education, career, and financial status; define your personality traits
and the nature of the relationships you enjoy; and write of the
accomplishments, exploits, talents, and skills you have mastered. Here are some sample sentences:

- She was promoted six times in two years to become division
  manager, faster than anyone in company history.

- He can charm an audience better than an Indian fakir does
  a snake.

- Their marriage was stronger and more passionate than any
  in a romance novel.

Describe your life as you would like it to be. If you placed
no limits on yourself, what would your life be like? Write of
your dreams and aspirations, and include every idea that occurs
to you—no matter how outrageous. How do other people view
you? Describe the impact you have on your friends, your family,
and the world. Even if you think you may never be able to
accomplish a goal, write it down. You may surprise yourself.

5. *Extract your goals from your biography.*   Read your biography
to determine the goals you have written down. Here are some
examples that may assist you:

    1. Achieve a net worth of $1,000,000.00
    2. Appear on a TV quiz show
    3. Learn to speak Spanish
    4. Travel to all fifty states
    5. Become a mother of three children
    6. Teach a class
    7. Meet a U.S. president
    8. Earn a college degree
    9. Hold public office
   10. Act in a play
   11. Write a book
   12. Attend the Superbowl, World Series, or NBA Finals
   13. Sew a gown
   14. Learn to ski, fly, ~~or sail~~ *dance, swim*
   15. Take a cruise
   16. Become district manager for my company
   17. Double my income
   18. Start my own business
   19. Climb a mountain
   20. Become a movie star.
    Drive a racecar

None of these goals are impossible; none of yours are either.
If you question whether something you have written is a legit-
imate goal or idle fancy, take a few minutes to visualize yourself
accomplishing it. If you can at all picture it and you are happy
with the outcome, then by all means write it down. If you can
not picture yourself accomplishing the goal or feel uncomfortable when you do picture it, leave it off the list for now.

This list is dynamic. You may add to it or subtract from it at any time. In order for your list to be effective you must review it at least once a week, if not daily. You acquire points each time you review the list and picture yourself accomplishing the goals set forth in it.

6. *Make plans to achieve your goals.* It is important that you establish interim steps which will lead you to your ultimate goals. "The journey of a thousand miles begins with a single step." Write one-month, one-year, and five-year plans for each of the items on your list. These are your road maps to success which will provide your subconscious with direction and aim for your life. For each step, make a clear, definitive statement about yourself as if you already have achieved it. Here is an example:

- June 1, 1996. I have earned a Bachelor of Arts degree in Psychology.

  - One month: I have selected a college and enrolled in two night school classes. I have requested my high school transcripts to be sent to my college. I have filed for the tuition reimbursement plan where I work.

  - One year: I have completed 12 units of on-campus work toward my degree. I have gained an additional 12 units through passing CLEP tests. (College Level Examination Program: This is a testing program designed to grant college credits for knowledge gained through reading and life experience. See your local college guidance office for details.) I have purchased a word processing system to assist me in writing the papers required.

  - Five years: I have earned 90 units toward my degree. Most of the classes I am now taking are in my major.

The more specific you are in describing these goals, the easier it will be for you to visualize yourself accomplishing them. This will cause you to accumulate positive points very rapidly. Of course, you must review this list and imagine yourself as having already accomplished the goals. Christ taught us to pray and then act as if our prayers had already been answered. When you do this, you infuse your subconscious with as many positive points as if you had actually accomplished the goal. Your self-image becomes that of a person who has mastered his aim. Soon you will discover that you have in fact attained your goal and that it was easier than you originally thought it would be.

7. *Continue to review these goals and update them monthly.* For each goal, write a new monthly plan and adjust your one-year and five-year goals to coordinate with your progress. As you near an accomplishment, look back at the progress you have made from month to month. This will inspire you to greater effort and will infuse you with points.

8. *Create a wish book.* Cut out pictures that represent the goals you have and save them in a scrap book. These pictures can be from magazines, newspapers, or any other source. They should give you a visual sense of your goals. For example, if you want a new house, cut out pictures that are similar to your dream house and place them in your wish book. Then, when you review the book, picture yourself living in the house.

The wish book can contain anything which will prod you toward your goals. You can alter a newspaper headline to read: "(Your Name) Sells Building For $1,000,000." You can create your own headline on a piece of notebook paper; you can even take a picture of something you want.

If you are especially eager to achieve a certain goal, tape the picture to your refrigerator door or on your bathroom mirror.

Place it anywhere you will see it regularly. This will continually reinforce your desire within your subconscious.

Should you ever find yourself saying that you are unworthy of the goal when you look at the picture, stop immediately and reinforce the positive goals. Do this by picturing yourself achieving the goal or having the object you desire. Those feelings of unworthiness arise from your negative self-image. Work even harder to acquire positive points.

In the next chapter you will learn visualization and affirmation techniques to enhance your ability to set and achieve your goals. These techniques will also improve your point score, allowing you to feel more worthy of your aspirations.

CHAPTER SUMMARY

1. Your attitude controls more self-image points than does any other aspect of your life. A positive attitude will generate positive points.

2. Winners practice winning in all their affairs. You are a winner if you keep your word, do the right thing, eat properly, avoid sugar, are honest, work hard, practice temperance, are friendly, behave properly, don't procrastinate, and have an attitude of gratitude.

3. Life is more pleasant for winners. Success comes easily; they radiate health, power, and prosperity; people are attracted to them; and they are secure within themselves.

4. When you take a risk, you gain points.

5. Establish the habit of winning by generating victories. Start small and gradually increase your challenges.

6. Establish goals for yourself and work toward their achievement. Picture yourself succeeding.

7. Keep a wish book of the goals you wish to achieve and objects you wish to acquire.

5

More Points

D<small>O YOU WANT TO HAVE AN EXTRA EDGE</small> on gaining self-esteem points? The last two chapters demonstrated how you can gain points and avoid losing them through your normal daily activities. This chapter contains exercises designed to accelerate your progress. And please remember that it is progress that is important. While you may be striving for perfection, understand that you will not reach it. Therefore, be gentle with yourself. If you cannot practice all of the methods discussed here, or if you have a difficult time, take heart. Do what you are able, persevere, and maintain a positive attitude, and you will make steady progress accumulating points.

Visualization

The subconscious tallies the points sent it from the conscious. It is not aware of their original source. The points may be generated as a result of a real event or from the imagination. It matters not. It is only important to note that your conscious mind is the actual determinant of the points.

Effectively, visualization is the act of using your imagination while in a relaxed state. You can use visualization to experience events entirely within your imagination. Not only is it like taking a trip without the kids, it's like taking a trip without leaving your chair. You can fool your subconscious into adding points by merely imagining events as you would like them to be. While you are relaxed your subconscious is more sensitive to the suggestions sent it. In other words, you accumulate more points when you use your imagination while in a relaxed state than you would if you were tense. The use of visualization then is an effective method to use in your continuing efforts to accumulate points.

There have been remarkable results attributed to visualization. It has been used to treat cancer patients, many of whom claim that its use is the direct reason for their remission. Many of the patients relax, then imagine an army of miniature Pac-Man heads eating away at the cancer. While this may sound silly, it has been known to work miracles (see Simonton, Simonton & Creighton, 1980).

Most successful people use some form of visualization to prepare themselves for a new task. An entrepreneur may see herself as having attained a goal well in advance of the actual occurrence. An athlete may imagine hitting a home run by "seeing" the ball meet his bat and "feeling" the power being transmitted from his arms. He then steps to the plate and performs the feat just as he had visualized it. A single person may imagine all aspects of a married life and be well-prepared to meet, court, and wed a well-chosen mate. Each of them is creating success points with the power of his imagination. The mind is very powerful, and visualization is one of the best tools to tap its potential.

Several years ago there was a study done by psychologist R. A. Vandell. Volunteers were divided into three groups. Each group was asked to shoot basketball free throws and their scores were tallied. The members of the first group were then asked to refrain from practicing or even thinking about basketball for twenty days. Those in the second group practiced free throw shooting each day for the same twenty days. Members of the third group were asked to visualize themselves making free throws each day, but to refrain from any actual practice. After the three weeks, each group was scored again on their proficiency at the foul line. As was expected, the group which did not practice and did not think about basketball did not improve. The second group, which practiced regularly, of course improved. Remarkably, the group that visualized themselves practicing improved almost exactly as much as did the group that practiced (see Maltz, 1960).

Does visualization work? Prove it to yourself. Select several areas of your life in which you wish to improve. Write each goal on a separate 3 x 5 card. When you are ready to begin a visualization session, select one card as the subject of your visualization. Read the card and take a few moments to focus on your goal. Be clear on the outcome you desire. Find a quiet place where you will not be disturbed. Turn on the answering machine or unplug the phone. Darken the room. Play music if it will help you relax and not be distracting. Find a comfortable chair, but not one in which you are likely to fall asleep. Sit. Place both feet on the floor and uncross your arms. Let your hands rest comfortably in your lap.

I suggest that you create a personal visualization tape to facilitate the relaxation and imaging processes. You may create your own script if you so desire, or you may use the following suggested steps. Whether you use your own script or the one below, speak softly into a tape recorder in a slow monotone. Avoid any dramatic inflection that may tend to stimulate rather than relax. Include soft background music on the tape, or merely play some at the same time you play your personalized tape. If you find the music distracting, discontinue its use.

Begin. Press play and record on your recorder and allow it to wind past the tape leader. You should use a tape that has at least thirty minutes to a side. Read your script or the following:

I am now entering into a visualization session to improve the quality of my life and gain self-esteem points. I will remember to picture my desires as if they were already available to me. I know I have the power to reach any goal.

I close my eyes and relax. I take a deep breath in through my nose for a count of 4. 1...2...3...4. I hold for a count of 4. 1...2...3...4. Now I exhale through my mouth for a count of 8, relaxing as I breath out. 1... 2... 3... 4... 5... 6... 7... 8. Again. I breathe in through my nose ...1... 2... 3... 4. I hold ...1... 2... 3... 4. Now I exhale and relax ...1... 2... 3... 4... 5... 6... 7... 8. Once again. I breathe in through my nose ...1... 2... 3... 4. I hold it ...1... 2... 3... 4. Now I exhale and relax ...1... 2... 3... 4... 5... 6... 7... 8.

I relax each part of my body. First my toes. I tense them for a few seconds ...1... 2... 3... 4. Release. I feel my toes relax.

Next I tense my calves ...1:.. 2... 3... 4. Release. I feel my calves relax.

Now my thighs. Tense ...1... 2... 3... 4. Release. Relax.

Now my buttocks. Tense ...1... 2... 3... 4. Release. Relax.

I tense my fingers ...1... 2... 3... 4. Release. Relax.

I move to my wrists and forearms. Tense ...1... 2... 3... 4. Release. Relax.

Now my upper arms and shoulders. Tense ...1... 2... 3... 4. Release. Relax.

I proceed to my neck. Tense slightly ...1... 2... 3... 4. Release. Relax.

Next I clench my jaw and lightly tense my facial muscles ...1... 2... 3... 4. Release. Relax.

Finally, I tense my stomach and chest ...1... 2... 3... 4. Release. Relax.

I feel myself in a deeply relaxed state.

"My body is filled with helium. I am light....so light. I feel myself floating away. I feel so relaxed. (Pause for 10 seconds)

My body is filled with lead. I feel myself sinking into the chair. Down....Down....Down. I feel so relaxed. (Pause for 10 seconds)

My joints are loosely held together with string. The strings are loosening even more. I feel all my joints relax. I am so relaxed. (Pause for 10 seconds)

I am now going to count backward from 10 to 1. As I count I feel myself becoming more and more relaxed with each number. With each number I will be more relaxed than I have ever been before.

10. My heartbeat is calm and regular. (Pause)

9. My breathing is soft and regular. (Pause)

8. I am very relaxed. (Pause)

7. Deeper and deeper. (Pause)

6. More and more relaxed. (Pause)

5. Deeper and deeper. (Pause)

4. I am calm and relaxed. (Pause)

3. Deeper and deeper. (Pause)

2. My entire body is relaxed. (Pause)

1. Deeper and deeper. (Pause)

I am now more relaxed than I ever have been. Each time I do this exercise, I will go deeper and deeper and will be more and more relaxed.

I am now ready to do my visualization. I am ready to picture in my mind the goal I have chosen for this session. I will remember details, sights, sounds, smells, and feelings. I will vividly see the expression on other peoples faces as I accomplish my goal. I will enjoy the feeling inside as I achieve my desire.

I will now be silent as I visualize. (Pause for 10 minutes or longer)

.

.

.

.

.

It is now time to return.

(Note: At this time you may wish to insert positive affirmations on your tape to amplify your visualization.)

Say: "I will now affirm my goals and commitment. I will repeat these phrases."

(Recite the affirmations, pausing between each to allow yourself to repeat the statement.)

Examples:

"I attract a loving relationship into my life."

"I radiate confidence and good cheer."

"I attract money and prestige to myself."

(You may include several affirmations, but they should be related to a single theme.)

(Regardless of whether you include affirmations, end the session with the following:)

I am now ready to return to full consciousness.

I will count up from 1 to 5. At each number I will be more fully alert and awake.

1. I feel myself beginning to stir.

2. I am becoming aware of my surroundings.

3. I move my feet and hands.
4. I stretch and move around.
5. I open my eyes. I am alert and awake, and I feel
marvelous.

Use your tape as often as possible as it is an easy way to gain points and relax at the same time. Here are some hints to improve the quality of your visualization:

1. *Live the event as though it were occurring now.* What is happening? What do you see? What do you hear? Are there any smells? How do you feel? What decisions can you make about yourself as a result of this event?

2. *Imagine the event as you want it to be.* Visualize yourself achieving success. Feel the joy of victory, of accomplishment, of a positive outcome. See your friends congratulating you. Tell yourself that you are a winner. Relax and enjoy the feeling for several minutes. Bask in the glory of your success. What positive decisions can you now make about yourself?

3. *Picture your visualization as though it would appear through your eyes.* In your visualization see the events unfolding before you. Live the event as though it were actually happening to you. Don't view the events as a spectator would. See through your eyes, feel through your body, taste with your mouth, smell with your nose, and hear through your ears.

4. *Use all of your senses.* The more senses you can involve, the more vivid will be the experience, and the more points you will accumulate. Therefore, include sight, sound, smell, touch, and taste as much as you can.

5. *Use your emotions.* The more emotional the experience, the more impact it will have on the subconscious, and, you guessed it, the more points you will gain.

If you have any difficulties becoming relaxed, if you struggle at visualizing yourself achieving your goal, or if your mind wanders, don't despair. Visualization requires practice. The more you practice, the better you will become. Once you become proficient, you will be able to relax at will. The images will be vivid and lifelike. You will send your subconscious points. You will improve your self-image, acquire a winning attitude, and achieve your goals.

The practice of visualization need not be limited to attaining your goals. You can also use it to re-live past events, aid in healing, reduce pain, overcome fears, and generate creative thoughts.

1. *Re-living past events.* Through visualization it is possible to re-live a past event and compensate for any point losses you may have stored as a result of the incident. Place yourself in the relaxed state. Imagine an event from your past. Picture yourself as you looked at the time. What clothes did you wear? What was your hair color and style? Who were your friends? Where were you?

Imagine the event as it occurred. How do you feel? Be as specific as you are able, even if you become uncomfortable. What decisions have you made about yourself as a result of this event?

Relax. Consciously reduce any tension you may have by repeating the relaxation techniques.

Use your imagination to minimize the event. Change the image from color to black and white. See it as shrinking away to nothing. Picture yourself erasing it from your mind. Write a word or words which represent the event on an imaginary chalkboard. See yourself using a chalk eraser and wiping it off the slate.

Next, re-create the event as you would have liked it to have occurred. Picture yourself achieving a positive outcome. See your friends' admiration for your skill and poise. Enjoy the warm feeling of having done well. Now, what positive decisions can you make about yourself?

Return to your awakened state with the feeling that you are free of one more negative event from your past. If you are still uncomfortable with the memory of the event, repeat this exercise. Do not re-live the negative event. Instead continue to re-create the positive outcome until it has entirely replaced the negative.

2. *Healing.* The next time you have a cut or scrape use visualization to aid in the healing. Place yourself in the relaxed state and picture the skin cells knitting together. See the wound healing. It may well speed your recovery.

If you are comfortable with using visualization on healing, you may wish to try it for all of your maladies. Ask your doctor's opinion of visualization for healing. Many in the medical profession are enthusiastic about visualization. Most important is your individual success. If it works for you, use it.

3. *Reduce pain.* You can use visualization to reduce or eliminate pain. Place yourself in the relaxed state. Imagine the pain as an object. Make it an amorphous glob. Give it a color. Picture the glob shrinking and fading in color until it completely disappears.

4. *Overcome fears.* It is possible to use visualization to face your fears and gradually overcome them. First, place yourself in the relaxed state. Next, picture yourself doing that which you fear. Perhaps you are afraid of heights. You can imagine yourself standing atop a tall building. Look down. When you experience the fear, consciously relax. Continue this for several sessions, until you are able to look down without becoming tense and fearful.

   If you are unable to relax at all when picturing yourself on top of a tall building, use the "mini-victory" method. Picture yourself standing on a step ladder or a footstool. Once you are able to master that height, gradually increase the challenge until you are comfortable at all elevations.

   The point is to visualize yourself doing what you fear, then consciously relax. You send positive points to your subconscious by telling it you are relaxed during a time when you were once fearful. When you actually stand atop a tall building, or face whatever fear it is you have, remember to relax, breathe deeply, and enjoy the view. You have conquered your fear and have gained self-esteem points.

5. *Generate creative solutions.* You can use visualization to generate creative thoughts and develop solutions to problems. Prior to placing yourself in the relaxed state, identify the issue. You should be able to state the problem and all its aspects. For example, you may be having difficulty paying your bills. That is the problem. Identify your income and enumerate your outgo. Be as specific as you are able.

   Now relax. When you achieve the relaxed state, let your thoughts flow. Do not attempt to visualize any solutions. Instead allow your own creative mechanisms to present you with a solution. Don't force it, just let it happen. Eventually a solution will appear if you relax and allow it to come.

You may even sleep on it. State your problem and be specific. Then just go to sleep. Forget the problem entirely and allow yourself a good night's rest. In the morning you may well awaken with a creative solution to your problem. You may even pop awake during the night suddenly struck with inspiration. Keep a note pad and pen or a tape recorder near your bed so you can immediately save your insights.

All of these applications of visualization create points. Reaching goals, re-creating the past, aiding healing, reducing pain, overcoming fears, and developing creative solutions have an obvious benefit. They also contain the by-product of making you feel better about yourself. When you feel good about yourself, you are guaranteed to generate points.

Once again, remember that the subconscious stores the messages sent from the conscious mind without editing them. It does not know if the original source of the message was from a real event or the result of the conscious imagination. To visualize success in a relaxed state is the equivalent of experiencing a successful event. The points stored in the subconscious will be the same as if you had actually experienced the event. As far as your subconscious is concerned, you have.

Prove to yourself this technique works. Generate some mini-victories using nothing but visualization. Perhaps you wish to lose weight but have been having a difficult time reducing. No matter what diet or exercise program you try, you are unable to drop more than a few pounds, which instantly return whenever you slip from your regimen.

Try visualization. Go easy at first and visualize the loss of five pounds. When you reach the relaxed state, picture yourself getting on a scale. See yourself weighing five pounds less than you do now. See yourself easily slipping into clothes that are a size smaller than what you currently wear. Imagine your body burning off excess fat cells. See the fat cells shrinking. Picture your friends commenting on your weight loss and asking you how you did it. Feel your joy at having lost the five pounds.

Make no other conscious changes in your life. Do not begin a new fad diet. Eat as you have been. Exercise as you have been. Continue your same lifestyle.

If you are diligent in your visualization, you will almost certainly see dramatic results. Without consciously changing your lifestyle, you will lose the weight. You may find yourself automatically exercising more and showing more restraint in your diet as a result of the visualization. If it feels natural, continue it. The point is to not discipline yourself. Just apply visualization to your weight problem.

If you are not overweight, find some other goal upon which to practice. Set a mini-goal and visualize its achievement. Do not change any other aspects of your life other than to visualize once or twice a day. Continue until you have achieved success. As you become more comfortable with visualization, you can apply it to more and more areas of your life.

Positive Affirmations

In Chapter 3 you were told how you lose self-esteem points through negative self-talk. When you say messages like, "I sure am dumb," or "I am as lazy as anyone I know," you are generating point losses just as if it were the result of an actual event. It is also possible, in fact desirable, to generate positive points through this very same self-talk. You can say, "I am an intelligent, ambitious person." As you say this, aloud or to yourself, combine it with strong positive emotion. Be forceful. Mean what you say. Feel the adrenalin flowing. The more emotion you put into the message the stronger the reinforcement is to the subconscious—the more positive points you will accumulate.

Practice affirmations in a way similar to what you did with visualization. Select an area of your life you wish to improve. Write several positive affirmations concerning this area. Remember to use positive, first-person statements, speak in the present tense, be brief, include a word which indicates a positive feeling, and be specific. Here are some examples:

- I am enjoying being a slim, trim 120 pounds. I maintain this ideal weight through a program of sensible eating and regular exercise.

- I love my job as a salesman. I enjoy calling on customers and providing them with service.

- I am poised and confident with members of the opposite sex.

- I enjoy being able to express myself clearly and demonstrate my fine mind and quick wit.

Make your own affirmation statements. Limit yourself to one or two categories at a time. For example, you may begin with weight and exercise. Once you have mastered these areas, you can expand to wealth and prosperity, then continue with loving relationships. Write each affirmation on a three-by-five card. Carry these cards with you. At free moments pull out a card and repeat the affirmation. Make sure that you add emotion to your statement as you say it. Feel the words and picture the results.

It does not matter whether you verbalize your affirmations, repeat them silently to yourself, or listen to them on tape. You will find that you are generating points in direct proportion to the number of times you repeat them and the strength of the associated emotion you place upon them.

You may even tape your affirmations, enabling you to listen to them while performing other activities. You may even play the tape while you sleep, which will have a tremendous impact. During sleep your subconscious is very receptive to suggestions. You have an opportunity to gain points very rapidly from your own self-talk.

To make a recording of your affirmations you obviously need a tape recorder and a blank tape. Arrange your three-by-five cards in the order you wish to say them. Turn on the recorder to record mode and wait a few seconds to allow the leader to feed through the machine. Enunciate your words clearly with feeling and emotion. Repeat each affirmation three times. Go on to the next one and continue until you are finished. If there is still room on the tape, start over again.

You are making your own tape so you can be as sophisticated as you wish. You may want to include music in the background. If so, either play the music while you are recording your affirmations or dub it in later. Select music that you believe is appropriate for your affirmations. I am not sure that the blues or some of the sadder country and western music would be appropriate. In my case, I like to use new wave, classical, or mellow jazz music. However, you be the judge. It is your tape.

Use Your Attention Units Wisely

We all seem to have a finite number of attention units. In other words, we can only deal with a limited number of issues at any given time. If you use your attention units wisely, you can enjoy life, continually gain points, and expand your capacity to experience life. In this manner you can gain more attention units.

Alas, most of us are not very intelligent in the application of our attention units and find we have less and less of them available as we age. We hoard these units by clinging to past events, hoarding grudges as if they were precious gems, tackling hundreds of projects we never have any intention of finishing, and committing ourselves to a plethora of thankless tasks better left to others or, even better, left alone. No wonder we never have the energy and drive to achieve all of the greatness for which we know we were destined.

There are a number of steps we can take to free our attention units for the important task of building a quality life:

1. *Reduce clutter.* In Chapter 6 there is a section on having a junkectomy. This is like an appendectomy, but instead of removing your appendix you remove unnecessary junk. Read the section and apply it. You will free several attention units.

2. *Complete unfinished business.* Complete all of your unfinished business. This can be accomplished by just doing the hanging task, such as filing those papers or fixing that faucet. It can also be accomplished by dropping it from your "To Do" List. Perhaps you don't really need to read that election pamphlet from three years ago or learn Spanish now that your cruise is over. Your subconscious demands completion. It devotes energy and attention units to every unresolved issue in your life. Therefore, the more unfinished business you retain, the less energy you will have for that which is truly important.

3. *Reduce your distractions.* Is it necessary to follow every sports event? Must you really watch television every night? Is the latest office gossip that important to you? Entertainment

is one thing, overindulgence another. You can easily free a number of attention units by reducing your reliance on these artificial stimulations. I have always been thankful to the NFL players and major league baseball players for their strikes of a few years ago. The absence of these televised sports weaned me from the habit of mindlessly following their activities. Whereas before I would spend many hours each weekend wasting my time, now I rarely watch a game. Instead, I enjoy the available attention units in ways which are much more rewarding.

4. *Close the past.* It is sad and wasteful to re-live over and over again negative events from the past. It may be instructive to profit from your mistakes, but it is unhealthy to dwell on them. Forget that dropped pass, lost love, or missed opportunity. They merely waste attention units and re-double the point loss already experienced.

Face Your Fears

You lose points each time you succumb to fear; you amass points whenever you face it head on. Eliminate a fear and you gain points while expanding your ability to deal with life. By eliminating a fear you emerge further from the shadows, and into the light and joys of life.

How then can you reduce or eliminate the fears in your life? Apply one or more of the following methods and watch your fears disappear; see your life become fuller and richer and gain points:

1. *Visualization.* Apply the methods discussed in the above section on visualization. This is a healthy and safe method

with which to begin. Through visualization you need only face the fear in your mind. This is where fear resides. So visualize attacking the problem on its own ground.

2. *Mini-victories.* Gradually desensitize your fears through mini-victories. If you are afraid of dogs, begin by looking at a picture of a dog and consciously relaxing. Next go to a pet store and look at the puppies in their cages behind the glass windows. Come in contact with a puppy or small, docile dog. Relax and breathe normally. Don't hold your breath. Continue to gradually increase your challenges until you are able to eliminate the fear entirely.

   Remember to keep a positive attitude and to appreciate your progress. Identify with the distance you have traveled, not how much of the journey remains. Perhaps you were once terrified of dogs and trembled at the sight of one. Now you are merely afraid but able to control your trembling. Rejoice, you are getting better.

3. *Talk about it.* Discuss your fears with an understanding person, either a close friend or a professional counselor. Find someone who will listen and sympathize. Avoid one who tells you how foolish your fear is. You will only lose more points and reduce your self-esteem further.

   By talking about your fears with a friend you begin to face the real issues. A problem shared is a problem halved. You may even discover the underlying reason behind the fear. Often the fear is real but the initial cause is no longer operative. Realizing this will help you overcome the fear.

   I used these methods to overcome my fear of joining a health spa. I had once been an athlete, but years of dissipation had deteriorated my physical condition. Friends suggested that

I join an exercise club to improve my fitness. I couldn't. I felt embarrassed just thinking about facing all of these beautiful bodies and the judgments they would make of me. I rationalized that all of the members were hedonistic, self-centered, and arrogant. Rather than admitting I was afraid to go, I painted all of the health clubs in the world with the broad brush of phoniness. I did want to improve my fitness however.

I began to exercise at home. I bought a set of weights, a small bench, and a jump rope. Three times a week I exercised by myself in my garage. In addition, I walked my dogs for a mile, or even two, every day. Gradually, my tone improved and my weight stabilized. These mini-victories bolstered my confidence. I was now able to admit that I feared joining a health club. This was an improvement over my previous rationalization that they were all inhabited by fitness freaks. The truth was that I was worried about how I would fit in—the fear of looking foolish.

As I continued making progress in my fitness, I began to wish I had more equipment available to me. I wanted an exercise bike, a rowing machine, even a sauna in which to relax after my workouts. Unless I joined a health club, this fitness craze of mine was going to get very expensive.

That is when I began to wish I could feel comfortable at a fitness center. I began to visualize myself joining one, and attending it regularly. At first, I only visualized myself taking some of the aerobic classes. I soon increased my imagery to include use of all the facilities. While I was doing this, I continued to exercise, which improved my fitness, which added points to my self-image.

I reviewed my goals, and added joining a health spa to my one-year goals. I wrote affirmations and repeated them regularly. I even cut out a picture of a health spa from a newspaper ad and placed it on my refrigerator.

One day three of my friends called within a single hour. They each informed me that the club at which they were members was offering a special incentive for new members. For one day only, their club would waive the standard initiation fee for anyone who wished to join. The only requirement was that I pay but a single month's fee. I could quit at any time with no further financial obligation. In spite of some remaining misgivings, I joined.

At first, I only visited at off hours when few people were there. Even then, I only rode the stationary bike and used the rowing machines. Still, I found the people there to be friendly and helpful. Some even volunteered to explain the use of other exercise equipment. Whenever I felt tense or nervous, I consciously relaxed and enjoyed the surroundings. After a few weeks I took the free fitness evaluation. The lady conducting it was extremely helpful. She tested various aspects of my fitness, reviewed each category with me, and recommended a program tailored to my lifestyle and needs. She patiently explained the use of the various machines and guided me through each exercise.

I now exercise regularly at this health club. The people there are generally much nicer than I had originally feared. All are polite and share knowledge and experiences. I gain points from exercising and from associating with others who are involved in fitness. I overcame a fear and gained points doing it.

Do you see the various methods I used to overcome my fear? I gained confidence through mini-victories. I acknowledged my fear. I set a goal and visualized its success. I strengthened the goal through affirmations and through a picture of my desired outcome. Each time I felt the fear, I consciously relaxed, thereby desensitizing myself to it. I gradually increased my involvement, emerging further from the shadows into a continuing pleasurable adventure.

Try these methods on your fears and watch them disappear. The points you gain will permeate all aspects of your life.

Develop a Sense of Humor

Life is better for those who don't take themselves too seriously. If life is to be enjoyed, a healthy sense of humor is an essential ingredient of that joy. You can easily improve the quality of your life if you can find a way to laugh at your troubles. Later in the book there is a chapter on support groups. Many of the better ones encourage their members to find amusement in their plight. They laugh together, not at each other.

Laughter has healing powers. Norman Cousins was diagnosed to have a terminal disease. In his book, *Anatomy of an Illness* (1979), he tells how he was told to arrange his affairs as he would be dead in less than a year. Instead of accepting the doctors' verdict, he decided to live. He bought a projector, and several Laurel and Hardy and Marx Brothers movies, and watched them regularly. The effect was remarkable. He literally laughed himself to health. He lived for several more years and toured the country lecturing on his success. Instead of being sickly, he was a vibrant, dynamic human who enjoyed life and truly appreciated the value of a sense of humor.

You too can take advantage of the curative effects of a good sense of humor. If you are able to laugh at yourself in a healthy manner, you will accumulate points. Well-applied humor reduces the tension in any circumstance. It tempers bad situations and enhances good ones. Laughter even releases positive endorphins in the brain. You feel better physically when you laugh.

Do yourself a favor. The next time you are sad or angry, take a few seconds to find some humor in the situation. Surely there is something funny about it. You will gain points and feel better.

Keep a Journal

A healthy discipline is to keep a written journal of your thoughts and actions. It will ensure a regular flow of positive points. You will be able to chart your progress and review your thoughts and feelings at various stages of your life.

Your journal can be your private storehouse representing your inner self. You need not show it to anyone. Before writing in your journal, find a quiet place where you can be alone. Relax for a few minutes. Now write. Avoid editing. Be spontaneous. It is not important if the words and phrases make sense. Punctuation is not important. Just write what you feel. Often you will be surprised at the results. Thoughts and emotions you have been suppressing may come tumbling forth. Do not despair. This can be very therapeutic and will enable you to gain insights into issues that have been motivating you without your being consciously aware.

If you have a difficult time starting, you can write of the day's events. They need not be anything significant. It is enough to write that you awoke earlier than usual, or even that you arose at the same time as every other day. Once you have completed your day's activities, you can review them. What did you feel about each event? Are you satisfied with your participation? Where have you gained positive points? What could you have done better?

Use the margins, write between the lines already written, use the back of the page. This is your journal. You will not be graded for neatness. The only grade you will ever get is based upon the quality of your life. The journal is a tool to aid you in improving your life. Use it as such. Express your inner self to your consciousness. You'll be surprised at what you discover.

Practice looking for positive outcomes. Every event in your life can have a positive outcome if you look for it. It may be that you learned never to do it again. Offer yourself suggestions on how you could improve your performance or your attitude.

Your journal is also a vehicle to aid you in charting your progress. It enables you to view your thoughts and feelings in retrospect. Perhaps there was a situation which you handled poorly last month. This month you encountered a similar event, but this time you were great. You can see what you've learned from the process of keeping a journal.

Chart Your Progress

Sometimes we get discouraged and think we are not making any progress in our goals or in the quality of our lives. If you chart your progress, you can easily note your improvements and congratulate yourself on the advancements you have made. Charting your progress is a great tool for overcoming discouragement. You can use your journal and record any positive advancements you have made toward your goals. You may count the number of days since you last had a cigarette or even chart how you are reducing your consumption. You may count the number of times you've exercised. You may count the compliments you've received since you began your growth process. Chart your progress and see your point score grow.

Live in the Here and Now

Most of us spend our time elsewhen. We are either reliving some past event or planning for a future one. We rarely spend time in the present moment. Those who are truly alive are able to pay attention to what is happening right now. This requires practice—a great deal of practice.

Here is a simple technique to bring you back to where you really are. Concentrate on your surroundings. Is the room warm? Is it night or day? Is the chair comfortable? What color are the walls? Continue until you are completely aware of your surroundings. Can you hear anything? Do you smell anything? What are you feeling right now? When you are doing this exercise, you may be reminded of something that occurred in the past or of something you are planning to do. Your mind may run with that for a while. When you become conscious that that is what you are doing, gently return to the present.

It doesn't matter what you are doing—it can be a pleasure if you pay attention. This is how to maximize the points in any situation. Live it and enjoy it. To illustrate, here is a quote from a Buddhist practitioner:

> There are two ways to wash the dishes. The first is to wash the dishes in order to have clean dishes, the second is to wash the dishes in order to wash the dishes. If while washing the dishes we think only of the cup of tea that awaits us, thus hurrying to get the dishes out of the way as if they were a nuisance, then we are not washing the dishes to wash the dishes. What's more, we are not alive during the time we are washing the dishes. In fact, we are completely incapable of realizing the miracle of life while we are standing at the sink. If we can't wash the dishes, chances are we won't be able to drink our tea either. While drinking the tea, we will be thinking of other things, barely aware of the cup in our hands (Farber & Fields, 1988).

Get the point? To be truly alive we must be present.

CHAPTER SUMMARY

1. Use visualization to aid you in achieving your goals. Practice the relaxation techniques and use your imagination. Don't be discouraged; it will take many sessions before you are proficient.

2. You can use visualization to relive past events, aid in healing, reduce pain, overcome fears, and generate creative thoughts.

3. Practice positive affirmations. Use the first person singular and the present tense. For example you may say, "I am healthy and fit. I practice good nutrition and exercise regularly."

4. Learn to face your fears through visualization, desensitization, and mini-victories. Chart your progress to prove to yourself that you are less fearful.

5. Develop a good sense of humor. It will temper negative points and enhance positive ones.

6. Keep a private journal. Record your intimate feelings and thoughts. Use it to evaluate your points and to evaluate your performance.

7. Learn to live in the present moment. That is the only time you are truly alive.

6

Overcoming Negative Experiences

D O YOU BELIEVE YOU HAVE ALREADY AMASSED a tremendous deficit of self-esteem points? Don't despair. It is possible to compensate for past point losses by balancing them with new point gains. It is even possible to view your history in a different perspective, thereby replacing the negativity with a newer point of view. To accomplish this requires diligence, but the results repay the effort a hundredfold.

Write an Autobiography

The first step to reducing your past point losses is to identify them. Over two thousand years ago Plato stated that an un-examined life is a waste. Nothing has changed to make that any less true today. To truly improve your self-image you must make the effort to understand your life. The best way to accomplish this is to review your past. Understand the patterns in your life and relate them to any point losses you suffered in years past. Unless you break past associations, you will act according to these decisions you made about yourself when you were a child—even if they no longer apply, or even worse, never were valid.

Anthony Robbins (1989), the charismatic founder of Robbins Research International, said that your past does not equal your future. He is absolutely correct, but only if you break the patterns that are compelling your behavior. The best way to identify your habit patterns is to write an autobiography in which you review your entire life with the goal of looking for repetitive behavior. An autobiography is essential to correcting any old negative patterns and reinforcing positive ones.

How do you begin? What should you say? What format should you use? How long should it be? How long should you take to do it? Here are a few suggestions:

1. Look upon it as an adventure. Plan to enjoy the experience.

2. Begin with your earliest recollections.

3. Write about your life. Write of events you remember in chronological order. Anything that occurs to you must have some significance, so write about it.

4. Say something about each year of your life. Some questions you may ask yourself to prod your memory are:

   • Who were the significant people in your life during that year? Examples are parents, friends, relatives, teachers, co-workers, bosses, and mates.

- What were the personally significant events which occurred in that year? Examples are school, jobs, marriage, divorce, moving, birthdays, and holidays. An event is significant if you say it is. Therefore write about taking the cat to the vet if you find it significant.

- Who did you resent or hate? How were you wronged?

- Who did you love or admire? How were you helped and who helped you?

- To whom did you cause harm? How did you wrong others?

- Who did you help?

- How did you cause harm to yourself?

- What decisions did you make about yourself as a result of these significant events?

5. Look for patterns. What events do you continually repeat with a different cast of characters? Are you repeatedly attracted to the same type of man or woman? Do you regularly have the same results? Do you always have problems with authority figures? Are your finances always in disarray? And, do you continually encumber more debt each time you get a raise? Identify all events that prove you are in a rut.

6. Don't ignore the pain. You may recall an event which brings you emotional pain. Allow yourself to experience the pain and identify your feelings for inclusion in the text. If the memory is too painful to face, write what you are able, then stop for a time. Do some activity which will divert your attention and with which you can gain positive points. Return to your writing as soon as you are able. This

will prevent your subconscious from magnifying the impact of the event even more.

These painful memories are very significant. Each of
them has had a major impact on your self-image. You must
do whatever is required to deal with these issues. Visualize
a happier outcome and forgive those who have harmed you.
If your painful memories linger, please seek professional
help. There are psychiatrists, psychologists, counselors,
priests, rabbis, and ministers trained to be of service to you.
Use them.

7. Devote as much time as your life merits. You don't have to
    rush. It is not a timed test. Be as thorough as you are able
    with each significant event.

8. Carry a pocket notebook with you. Use it to write signifi-
    cant events as they occur to you during the day.

9. Be honest. Without the courage to face reality, life is
    meaningless. Write what really occurred, not how you tell
    the story to others in order to protect your image.

10. List your accomplishments and assets. How have you
    helped people? What have you done well? Describe those
    events when you gained points. As you write of your
    victories, relive them and enjoy the memories. This will
    give you strength to face the negatives.

Once you have completed this phase of your autobiography
you are ready to begin an analysis of your life. Review your life
and identify the negative and the positive. You are determining
your life score to date. Consider the following categories:

1. *Patterns.* What patterns recur frequently in your life? When did you first begin each pattern? What initially caused you to react as you do? What can you do to break the pattern? Remember you can change any pattern by using the tools of visualization, mini-victories, positive actions, affirmations, and correct attitude.

2. *People who have harmed you.* List all of the people you believe have wronged you. If you feel or felt any anger or resentment toward them, add them to the list. Alongside each name write a very brief description of the act they did to harm you. If you can't remember a name, or never knew it, write something which will guide you to identifying the person.

3. *People whom you have harmed.* List all of the people to whom you have caused difficulty. Don't rationalize or excuse your behavior. Write a complete and thorough list. Use names, or descriptions, and add a brief summary of the harm you have caused.

4. *Undesirable characteristics.* List all of your traits which you dislike or believe are causing you grief. These may be such items as greed or lust, or that you are always late, or that you are insincere. Be honest. Your subconscious has already adjusted your score for each of these traits, so there is no reason to minimize them now.

5. *Assets.* Don't forget the positive. Identify everything which you consider an asset. List every victory, success, kindness given or received, accomplishment, and happy memory that occurs to you. Include moments of joy and those

unplanned but pleasant events that hold a special memory for you. Be especially mindful of those characteristics you possess which make you a special person. Identify those traits you like most about yourself.

Tell It to Someone

It is now time to confirm your judgment. You will get another's perspective of your life story. The best way to determine if you have made an accurate assessment of your life is to read your autobiography to another human being—preferably someone who knows you well. Another person may be able to offer you insights about yourself that you can't or won't recognize. "Oh, if we had the gift God gae us, to see ourselves as others see us," penned Robert Burns in his poem "Ode to a Louse." What he means is that we often see ourselves in an entirely different perspective than do others.

It is okay to use a priest, minister, or therapist if you are skittish about revealing personal intimacies to a loved one. Select your confessor wisely, however. It is important to receive feedback either from someone who knows you or from someone who is at least knowledgeable about human behavior.

I have done this exercise three times. Each time has been a valuable and rewarding experience. The first time I wrote an autobiography was in a college class for adults returning to school to complete their degrees. On the first draft, I was reluctant to reveal much about myself. I felt the professor had no right to know any intimate details of my life. Therefore, I initially wrote of only the most trivial events. However, as I considered the assignment, I realized it could offer a great deal of merit to me. I became eager to tell everything. I exposed my fears and weaknesses, and shared my triumphs and successes. I relished the opportunity to write about myself. This second draft was long, disjointed, and marvelous. Still being reluctant to fully expose myself, I edited the final version, but kept the full exposé.

During the latter part of the semester I had an opportunity to discuss my autobiography with the professor. He was quite receptive, which gave me the courage to read him my long version. As I read, he offered insights and observations which I hadn't considered. Many times, when I had condemned myself for some foolish act, he was able to suggest an alternate point of view. Often his perspective revealed that I had been overly critical of myself.

When we were finished, I felt lighter and more carefree. Indeed, I was. I had just dumped a tremendous emotional burden. I felt good about myself and gained many points in the process.

Each of the next two times I wrote an autobiography, I gained additional insights into my character and into my self-image. I gained inner strength which enabled me to face personal issues I had previously avoided. I noticed destructive patterns in my life and was able to take action to avoid repeating them. I was able to identify lingering anger and resentments, and was also able to release them. I also discovered assets I had ignored and was able to hone them for greater benefit to my self-image. As a result of each of these efforts my life improved in ways I had hardly dared imagine. I was buoyed by the effort to take more risks and expand my personal and professional life. I believe I was compensated a hundredfold for the effort I invested.

Compensating for Lost Points

Now that you have an honest appraisal of yourself, you can set out to compensate for any negativity you may have accumulated during your lifetime. Use the lists you made when analyzing your autobiography. Add and correct them based upon the feedback you received when you told your story to an understanding friend. Use the following suggestions to gain points from your prior negative experiences:

1. *Review your patterns.* You identified the patterns in your analysis, now correct them. First, determine what triggers you to revert to a pattern and what reward you obtain from using one. Perhaps you once disrupted a classroom with your antics and were rewarded with the laughing approval of your classmates. Now you find you always contribute levity to all meetings you attend—even when it is upsetting and inappropriate. You associate the reward from the past with a present event, even if it is no longer productive to do so. Become aware of whenever you are doing something that fits one of your old, destructive patterns. When you have this awareness, take steps to alter your usual actions. This will begin to break the pattern.

   Practice breaking all patterns. For example, alter your morning routine. If you shower, then eat breakfast, reverse the sequence. Take a new route to work and change the route weekly. Get your brain functioning in an aware state and stop operating on automatic pilot.

   Visualize different outcomes for your usual patterns. Use mini-victories to gain positive points and the confidence that you can change. Determine when you first began your pattern. What caused you to follow the pattern? Does it still apply? Visualize that original event differently to compensate for the original point loss.

Use affirmations to replace points that were previously lost. If your pattern is to leave a job after a year, develop an affirmation such as, "I am a career-oriented person. I am a loyal employee."

2. *People who have harmed you.* Make an effort to forgive everyone on the list. If you are spiritual or religious, pray for them. At first, don't try to understand their motives. Just stop holding a grudge. Grudges are heavy and burdensome things. Lighten your load. Many of the people on the list will be easy to forgive. Their transgressions will have occurred years ago and no longer have much impact on you. Nevertheless, say aloud, "I forgive this person for having caused me problems." Use the name and be specific about the events. Repeat the process until you can say it without feeling anger.

For those against whom you harbor deep or recent hurts, it may take more effort. Try the forgiveness statement first. If that does not seem to work, take the following actions:

- Realize that every resentment you have is taking up space in your mind and costing you points. Is it worth the price to hold onto your righteous anger?

- Depersonalize the issue. Did they harm you intentionally? If not, why are you taking it so personally? If they did deliberately set out to cause you pain, determine what could have motivated them. Was it jealousy? If so, they are to be pitied, not reviled. Was it fear on their

part? Once again, they are to be pitied. If you examine
their motives you will find that they have probably
reacted through greed, anger, or fear. You are resentful
toward someone who hasn't the self-esteem to have
reacted any differently. Why carry these burdens with
you? They are not worth it.

3. *People you have harmed.* You have identified all of the people
for whom you have caused difficulty. Set about to correct
your own transgressions. Determine how you can compensate for what you did. If you owe money, pay it back. Be
anonymous if you must, but return the money. If you have
insulted a person or assassinated his character, face him and
apologize. If you have lied or cheated to reach a goal, take
action to compensate those of whom you took unfair
advantage.

Don't avoid this process by finding fault with the
others. Don't tell yourself that they deserved it. Perhaps
they did, but you are trying to compensate for your lost
points, not theirs.

4. *Undesirable characteristics.* Identify the reverse side to every
negative trait that you have identified. If you are constantly
tardy, emphasize the need to be prompt. Work to replace
each of your negative characteristics with a positive one.
Cultivate these positive traits and soon the negative will
be supplanted. Use mini-victories and visualization to
begin your journey. Go easy. You will not change overnight. The key is that you now have a model of the behavior
you desire.

5. *Assets.* Your assets are the foundation upon which to build
your healthy self-image. Cultivate them, relish them, and
remind yourself constantly of how your life is better for

having them. Let your assets compound to gain even more points.

Reward yourself once you have completed your autobiography, reviewed it with another person, and analyzed it. Take a vacation. Buy yourself new clothes. Do something to affirm that you have done a wonderful feat. You have gained thousands of points by writing your autobiography and thousands more by revealing your life to another. Add to those points by rewarding yourself and letting your subconscious know that you are deserving of all that is good and wonderful.

Meditation

Another healthy method to overcome any negativity and to enhance your self-image is to practice meditation. Meditation is a great deal like guided imagery. The difference is that, instead of sending messages to your subconscious, you listen to it. You allow your subconscious to bring forth issues that you may consciously be ignoring.

To meditate you simply place yourself in a relaxed state as described in Chapter 5. You may want to play soothing music in the background. Make sure that any music you select is neither stimulating nor distracting. You may wish to light a candle and gaze at it until your eyelids droop and close gently. Do what you wish to create a proper setting in which to relax.

Many meditation practices involve continuously repeating a mantra. This is not necessary, even though it is certainly acceptable. You may find such repetition can help quiet your thoughts. In fact, that is the basic purpose of meditation. You want to stop any inner monologue you are experiencing, become still, and come to know the inner recesses of your mind. Meditation allows you to listen to the voice of your soul. While this voice is powerful and supportive, it is often overpowered by all the noise in your brain.

A simple method of using a mantra for meditation is to repeat a neutral word each time you exhale. The word should have no emotional attachments for you. For example, you may say, "OM," or "AH." You may even count your breaths by thinking or saying "one" on your first exhalation and "two" on your second. Continue until you reach "ten," then start over at "one."

I find it most effective to repeat "One" with each exhalation as I imagine my thoughts drifting through my mind like clouds crossing the sky. I don't dwell on any thought. Instead, I observe each as it passes and allow the next thought to waft into consciousness.

It is understandable and acceptable if you find your mind wandering or fixating on a specific thought. You may even find yourself thinking about work or your chores. That is okay. Those thoughts are in the forefront of your mind and will naturally float by at first. Allow them to pass and don't chide yourself for not thinking deep thoughts. However, if you become aware that you are dwelling on a thought, gently dismiss it and clear your mind by reciting your mantra, relaxing, or counting your breaths.

This gentle, relaxing exercise is very powerful. At times you may find yourself confronted with issues that you have long ignored or consciously forgotten. The subconscious does not ever forget. It reacts to matters regardless of your conscious efforts to ignore them. When you achieve a meditative state and allow your subconscious to talk with you, it may well bring forth these very problems. Listen. This is part of the process to recapturing those lost points.

Allow the subconscious to tell you what you are avoiding. These are the issues that are controlling your life and preventing you from succeeding. However, when these painful memories surface, do as you will with all meditative thoughts: gently dismiss them and clear your mind. It may be very difficult to do this, but keep repeating your mantra, relaxing, or counting until you are able to return to the relaxed state. When finishing the meditation write about these issues in your journal. Evaluate the meaning of your memories and experiences. How are you now being affected by them? What actions can you take to gain enough points to replace the negative images? Did your subconscious provide you with the solution when it presented the problem? Once you have decided on the proper course of action, use all of your tools of visualization, mini-victories, writing, talking to others, and affirmations to overcome these losses.

Meditate for at least ten minutes each day, preferably thirty. You will find that meditation can be more refreshing than sleep. This means you will require less sleep and be more efficient during your day when you meditate. Another way to look at meditation is that it energizes you enough to more than compensate for the time it requires to practice it.

You will also notice that you have more energy and are able to focus on tasks more readily. The rest of your life will improve if you practice meditation. Each time you meditate, you can chalk up points and relax while doing it.

Professional Help

It is possible that you may uncover some complicated issues in your life during meditation or when writing your autobiography. When certain issues come up, you may wish to seek the help of a trained mental health professional. There is no shame in this. After all, you go to a medical doctor to have your physical body checked. Why not give equal consideration to your mental well-being? Having problems doesn't mean you're crazy. Everyone has situations in their lives in which they could use the help of someone else. The next chapter discusses support groups. These are another source of assistance. However, you may wish to begin with a professional.

Select your counselor carefully. Find someone who can assist you with your problems and with whom you can be comfortable. You may be establishing a long-term relationship, so be diligent in your selection effort. Determine what approach will be used to deal with your issues. Is it something with which you will be comfortable? Do you believe the therapy will work?

Once you enter into therapy, commit yourself to it. You can gain points each session if you are honest and cooperative. Do yourself a favor and participate in your own well-being.

Junkectomy

As mentioned in Chapter 5 you can have a junkectomy to rid yourself of negativity and to free your attention units. A junkectomy is like an appendectomy. It is an operation to rid yourself of that which is no longer useful. A junkectomy clears space in your life. It frees you from many of the burdens of the past. This enables you to feel lighter and more energetic.

Begin a junkectomy by removing the clutter from your life. Literally clean your attic and closets of the junk you have collected. Do the same with your garage and cupboards. If you have anything that you haven't used for over a year, give it away, sell it, or dispose of it.

More significantly, get rid of those items for which you once had a strong emotional attachment, but which are now merely clutter. It takes honesty and discipline to free yourself from these burdens of the past. It may be a painful process. Do it anyhow, for the rewards are great.

My first junkectomy consisted of discarding old pictures, letters, and even newspaper clippings of my sports accomplishments. These mementos were very dear to me, but they no longer represented who I was. Many were unhealthy links with the past. Not all were painful memories, it is just that they were anchors which prevented me from moving forward. I cleaned house and made space for new possibilities. Almost immediately I established an enjoyable romantic relationship, made more money, and bought a new sports car. These items were more tangible and rewarding than the relics I had been saving.

Be ever vigilant of acquiring more junk. When you do, dispose of it immediately. These items always cost points if held too long. Life is to be lived in the present. Get rid of the junk that unhealthily links you to the past.

Let Go of the Past

Don't get stuck in the past. Have you ever noticed people who are stuck in an age or time? They still wear their high school sweater or dress, act and talk as though it were still the sixties. They continually relive the days of their greatest success—even though it was over twenty years ago. You can't proceed with life if you are unable to acknowledge your current status. You are a certain age in the current time and in a specific place. Live accordingly. You may have had a special time in your life, but if you want another one, you must begin by participating in today.

CHAPTER SUMMARY

1. Write your autobiography to determine your current score. Tell your story to another person to get a fresh perspective on your life.

2. Analyze your autobiography to determine any components which contribute to a negative self-image. Use visualization, meditation, self-talk, and mini-victories to help you overcome the negative.

3. Seek professional guidance to help unravel complicated issues in your life.

4. Meditate daily to listen to your subconscious.

5. Clear all the junk from your life. Reduce clutter. Let go of those mementos tying you to the past.

6. Learn to accept yourself as you are now and live in the present moment.

7

Support Groups

HUMAN BEINGS ARE NOT MEANT TO LIVE ALONE. Since the cave
dwellers gathered together for mutual protection, we have had
a need to be with other people. It is perhaps a residual of that
need for security that we tend to feel more comfortable with
people who are either a great deal like us or who offer us comfort
and solace. In many large cities there remain ethnic neighbor-
hoods for several generations after they were first formed by
immigrants. There is no prejudice associated with this phenom-
enon. It is merely more homelike for the residents.

Many of us have lost our sense of belonging and of community. We don't know our neighbors, our local officials, or even
the names of our elected representatives. We physically and
metaphorically surround ourselves with walls and fences to
protect our possessions and our feelings. We isolate to protect
our insecurities, rather than participate to feel included. Consequently we lack the real security, comfort, and solace that can
only be achieved within a group.

The opposite extreme is ultimately just as empty. We rush from place to place and from event to event at a frantic pace. We really don't take the time to form lasting alliances. Worse, we really don't get to know anyone nor allow anyone to truly know us. In a crowded and rushed society, we can easily find ourselves feeling isolated and lonely, while never actually being alone. We still need the comfort and security of others, but are too busy doing instead of being. To compensate for our feelings of emptiness and separation we redouble our activities or seek solace in drugs, alcohol, food, or possessions. Neither escapism nor frenzied activity gains us any points. In fact, they cost us a great many.

It is very unhealthy to seek comfort and peace of mind through point-depleting activities, escapism, or isolation. We are better served by selecting and joining a support group which will satisfy our needs for companionship and security, thereby offering point-enhancing opportunities. For some that means taking a risk to leave their isolation. For others it means reducing their activities to participate in something meaningful and valuable.

A well-chosen support group can provide great opportunities for growth and happiness. It can fill voids in your life and serve as a warm, secure environment. You achieve a special comfort by being associated with those who appreciate you and what you can offer. If you have been practicing this program of gaining self-esteem points, you will find you have a great deal to offer. You will surely have stories of success and growth which will inspire others.

Groucho Marx once remarked, "I would never join any organization which would have me as a member." With tongue in cheek he was saying that he was such a scoundrel that any organization which would accept him had such low standards as to be quite undesirable. I am sure Groucho Marx did not really feel that way about himself, and I hope you don't feel that way about yourself either. If you are reluctant to join a group, work on your self-image via other point-gaining activities. Soon you will be willing and eager to join with others to learn from them and share of yourself.

You are probably already a member of several groups. You may have a group of friends at work with whom you have lunch regularly. You are probably friendly with your neighbors—even if you don't socialize with them. You may be a member of a bowling or softball team. These types of groups can offer you companionship and a sense of belonging. They do not, however, necessarily offer you an opportunity to improve your self-image, grow, and thrive. These types of groups offer a social outlet which is good. They aren't typically classified as support groups, however. To truly achieve a high level of self-esteem you need a group which will nurture you with guidance and support.

Select your support group wisely. Make sure it offers you an opportunity to gain a sense of community and that it is compatible with your lifestyle. There are several criteria you should use to select a support group:

1. *Common Interests.* You will want to select a group with which you have common interests. You need not have the skills to immediately contribute, but you must have an interest in the activities of the group. In other words, you need not be a scholar to join a discussion group, you need merely have an interest in learning. Also, you need not share all interests with the other members. In fact, mutual caring and understanding can well serve as proper common interests.

2. *Purpose.* Your group should have a purpose. You should have a purpose for joining. Make sure your purpose for joining a group agrees with their purpose for being. Join Toastmas-

ters to gain poise and learn to speak in public, not to find new victims for your practical jokes.

There is always the additional purpose for all your activities—to gain self-esteem points. Therefore, make sure that membership in the group will be enhancing to your self-image.

3. *Supportive.* Make sure the group is supportive of you and your goals. Avoid those groups which practice demeaning rituals or which demand unhealthy allegiance. Instead, find an organization where you can be comfortable, accepted, and encouraged.

4. *Positive Value.* Find a group in which you can develop positive traits and gain points. The group should be one which encourages you to become more proficient or competent. They can do this by providing role models, formal and informal education, healthy activities, or a nurturing and challenging environment.

5. *Integrity.* The group must be honest, upright, and sincere if you are to gain self-esteem points from membership.

6. *Enjoyable.* The group should be one in which you enjoy being a member. If you like the group, you will participate more freely and feel more comfortable and secure.

7. *Responsible.* Absolutely avoid any group which encourages you to accept the role of a victim. No matter how well-meaning these groups may be, they will do nothing to further your self-esteem. In fact, most of these groups merely foster the agenda of their leaders at the cost of its members' self-esteem points. Find a group which takes

responsibility for itself and encourages you to do the same for yourself.

Examples of Support Groups

One of the finest organizations and social models to be developed in the twentieth century is Alcoholics Anonymous. The success of this fellowship has inspired over three hundred other associations who pattern themselves after A.A. and their 12 Step program of recovery. The only membership requirement A.A. has is that a person must have a desire to stop drinking. The members are from all races, creeds, and social levels. It is not unusual to find an executive and a street person sitting alongside each other at a meeting.

Alcoholics Anonymous rejects no one. They realize that they must help each other if any are to survive. As a part of this philosophy, they accept anyone wishing to join. In fact, there are no dues, fees, or initiations. A person is a member merely by saying he or she is a member.

They are self-supporting and refuse outside contributions, lest they be overly influenced by other interests. They decline to become involved with any politics, organization, or institution as it would detract from their purpose. They exist solely to help each other stay sober and carry their message to other alcoholics still suffering.

Attend an open A.A. meeting and see these people enjoying life. They are recovering from a disease which had robbed them of health and self-respect, yet they are now happy to be sober. Ask an A.A. member for help with your drinking problem and you will be amazed. He or she will probably spend hours with you trying to help. If you then reject the help, the AA'er will still be warm and will tell you that there is always a place waiting for you when you are ready. A major part of their recovery is helping others to recover. This is indeed a tremendous model for all support groups.

A.A. meets all of the tests for a support group. The members have the common interest of achieving and maintaining sobriety. It has the purpose of allowing its members to become functioning, productive members of society. The members are extremely supportive of each other. A major component of their philosophy and the basis for their founding is that one alcoholic can help himself stay sober by helping another alcoholic stay sober. They offer positive value in a number of ways, not the least of which is their 12 Steps. These steps are designed to lead the alcoholic toward recovery and a spiritual way of life (see Appendix A).

A.A. has unquestionable integrity and offers an enjoyable experience for its members. At an A.A. meeting a member receives support, understanding, and sympathy. The meetings are often punctuated with laughter as these fine people demonstrate their love for each other and their zest for life. Most members relish the prospect of going to a meeting where they can share with and care for their fellow alcoholics.

Of course, if you are not an alcoholic, it may be difficult to relate with other members of the organization. However, you may have other issues in your life which can be dealt with by an organization modeled after A.A. As mentioned above, there are over three hundred organizations based upon the Alcoholics Anonymous model. There are Overeaters Anonymous, Smokers Anonymous, Narcotics Anonymous, Adult Children of Alcoholics, Al-Anon (for those affected by the alcoholism of others), Co-Dependents Anonymous (for those unduly influenced by other people), Shoppers Anonymous, Workaholics Anonymous, Gamblers Anonymous, Sex Addicts Anonymous, and Neurotics Anonymous to name but a few. These support groups help each other to solve their common problems. If you suffer from any type of compulsive or obsessive behavior, there is probably a group which can offer you assistance and support. Look in a telephone directory for information on how to locate your support organization. If there is not an appropriate support group in your area, start one. You would do well to model it after A.A.

There are thousands of other groups with which you may find identification and support. Churches and other religious organizations are another type of group which can offer you opportunity for support. By definition, they are established to offer spiritual support, but most now offer much more. Set aside any prejudices and preconceived ideas you may have concerning organized religion. If you have been away from any organized religion for some time, or if you have never been associated with one, you may be pleasantly surprised. The common complaint of the sixties and seventies was, "I believe in God. I just can't stomach any organized form of worship. They seem so hypocritical."

This has changed greatly. Many religious organizations are responding well to the earthly needs of their congregation. They are offering help for the realities of living along with their own brand of eternal salvation. These churches and other religious groups now realize that they must provide guidance for the problems and issues of daily life if they are to survive. Many have responded admirably. Check out your old church and see if it now offers you the support and comfort for which you are looking.

There are now many "New Age" churches which seem to have emerged in the past few years. While many have been around for over a century, they are now receiving more recognition. These churches offer opportunity to come to terms with God in your own way. They offer classes in health, prosperity, and understanding the laws of the universe. Many are interested in astrology and other psychic phenomena. Once again, check them out and see if one has what you want. If you have any spiritual aspect to your life at all, there is certainly a religious organization to which you can comfortably belong.

If you have no compulsions and no desire to become a member of any organized religion, there are still thousands of opportunities for you to find a support group. The important issue is that you find some vehicle where you can gain self-esteem points from contact with other human beings, preferably while you enjoy yourself.

Investigate adult education classes such as sewing, cooking, crafts, hobbies, and self-improvement. Look into fitness clubs, diet support groups, science clubs for hobbyists, singles organizations, or couples groups. Offer your services to helping others in Big Brothers/Big Sisters, Goodwill, and any other community service group which accepts volunteers. Try helping those at Suicide Prevention if you want to feel grateful for your own conditions. Join the Eagles, Elks, Moose, or other fraternal organization. They are involved in many worthwhile services while offering a social outlet.

Become involved in the political process. Join a political campaign or work for an issue. Do something to support your country and your community.

Find some organization in which you feel a degree of comfort. Avoid any which will cause you to lose points. Beware of zealots and their cults. You are looking for support, not agony, fealty, or enslavement.

The idea is for you to get involved in something larger than yourself. You gain points just for making a commitment. If you wisely select the organizations you join, you will soon meet people in whom you can confide. They will help you to add perspective to the issues in your life. You further gain points by helping others. Much has been written in this book about compensating for any aspects of a negative self-image by acquiring points. The finest way to accumulate points is to remove the focus from yourself and place it on others. Your problems fade when you concentrate on offering support to other people. A country club may offer you the opportunity to be with others and gain points, but doing community service will pile them on.

Join an organization. Get involved. You owe it to yourself and to your community. Pay back some of the abundance you already have. We all have twenty-four hours each day. No one is more wealthy in time than is another. Spend some of your time to be with others and you will automatically gain points.

Selecting Your Support Group

Here are some suggestions to guide you in selecting a support group which is appropriate for you:

1. *Ask friends, neighbors, and co-workers.* One good source of information is your immediate associates. They know you and where your interests lie. They may understand you well enough to guide you toward a group which will suit your purposes and even fulfill needs they see in you but which you have yet to identify. They may also have enough sense to prevent you from joining an organization which would be detrimental to you, but to whose message you may be susceptible. Ask these people for suggestions. They may not only offer advice, but may well join with you.

2. *Find a group which can help you achieve your goals.* You have certain goals and objectives. Find a group which offers guidance and support toward these aspirations. You will obviously have common interests and may well meet many role models who are already doing that which you desire to do. For example, if you want to start a business, join an entrepreneurs club.

3. *Ask your role models.* Do you know people who you admire and wish to emulate? If so, ask them if they are a member of any organizations which have helped them to achieve their success. Take a risk. Ask, even if you have never met them. The answers and the results may surprise you. Many successful people are happy to share their success and to provide opportunity and information to others. Your role models may well introduce you to a support group which is perfect for you.

4. *Use the information from your autobiography.* During the process of writing and analyzing your autobiography you discovered your personality traits. You identified your defects and your assets. Use these lists to guide you to a support group. If you need help overcoming a major problem, find a support group that can assist you. For example, if you are shy, join Toastmasters. They can help you and will be supportive. If you have an asset which needs nurturing, find a support group in which you can develop further. If you are witty and clever and wish to gain even more poise, you may also be a candidate for Toastmasters.

   You may join an organization for any number of reasons or motivations. Make sure the group is able to offer you help. Also, make sure you can gain points from the experience.

5. *Take classes and lessons.* Taking a class in a subject which interests you may well lead to your discovering a valuable support group. I took scuba diving classes. This led to my meeting a group of people who became dear friends and proved to be very supportive. Together we formed a Master Mind Group (see Napoleon Hill, 1960) to assist each other in achieving our goals. Our initial common interest was scuba diving, but we have found many more common interests. In fact, each of us has broadened our lives by using the other members of the group as role models.

6. *Volunteer work.* Offer your help and support to others. This will add points and will introduce you to people who are as giving and caring as yourself. You can give and receive at the same time.

CHAPTER SUMMARY

1. End your isolation or reduce your frantic activity by joining a support group which will enhance your self-esteem.

2. Make sure you share common interests with a group.

3. Make sure you agree with the purpose for the group's existence.

4. Before you join, verify that they are supportive, offer positive value, and have integrity.

5. Make sure it is a group with which you will enjoy being associated.

6. Use your intelligence and the guidance of others to assist you in your search for a nurturing support group.

8

Love, Romance, and Points

ONE OF OUR GREATEST GOALS and one of the greatest rewards of a healthy self-image is to know romantic love. Few are happier or more alive than when they are in love. More songs are written about love than any other topic. More energy is placed in finding it than any other pursuit. We dream of love, talk of it, plan for it, and seek it with all the fervor we can summon. If we don't find it or it is unrequited, we fill our emptiness with food, drugs, alcohol, possessions, or promiscuity. Few of us understand the process by which two people meet and fall in love. All we know is that we want love and are willing to do practically anything to get it.

There are steps you can take to insure that you meet and attract someone with whom you can develop a strong romantic relationship. You truly can attract the person of your dreams. To realize your quest you must first build the self-esteem to attract such love. Make yourself worthy of love and it will find you. Remember, that perfect mate is seeking you even while you are seeking her or him. Use your energy to improve yourself. Not only is this the only way to find lasting love, it provides you with the strength of self-esteem to sustain your relationship once you have found it.

Steps to Attracting Love

If you are seeking a relationship, the following list of actions may guide you. Remember, WE GET WHAT WE BELIEVE WE DESERVE. Develop your own self-worth and your true love will appear like magic. Seek him or her before you are ready and you will only be disappointed. The quest for true love, like all other goals, begins from within.

1. *Giving and accepting love.* Do not so focus on finding a mate that you ignore the other relationships in your life. If you want to be able to give and receive love with just one man or woman, do not withhold it from all others. Change your focus to correct such an inappropriate approach to romance. Learn to love those already in your life. You may soon see that you have many dear friends for whom you care deeply. They probably love you as well and have demonstrated that love numerous times. Change your attitude. It may help you realize that you already have what you have been seeking. You have companionship and support. Every time you are a friend or allow someone else to be your friend, you gain points. This in turn makes you more worthy of a primary romantic relationship. Once you love others enough to believe you deserve it for yourself, you will find yourself happily involved with that special person of your dreams.

2. *Respect.* You simply and absolutely must respect members of the opposite sex. You may not think of yourself as a chauvinist—male or female, but examine your feelings very closely. In your mind are women and men different? Do you see them as schemers who take advantage of you? Do they fail to communicate properly and never keep commitments. Perhaps this is true for some of those you have known. It may even be true for all those you have ever dated. But, it is not true for all of them. The majority of all men and women are warm, sensitive human beings. They have feelings too and, like you and your friends, they are trying to survive in a sometimes hostile environment. Change your attitude lest you be another contributor to some of that hostility.

   You continually gain points when you respectfully listen to what someone, man or woman, has to say. You add to those points when you respond in loving ways. That does not mean that you must be obsequious or that you must subordinate your beliefs. It does mean that when you accept and respect each person, you grant yourself understanding and you gain points.

3. *Health and good looks.* You want a mate who is healthy and attractive. Big deal, doesn't everyone. If you are over-weight, ill-groomed, and forlorn how can you expect to attract your soul mate? Perhaps if you quit smoking; reduce your reliance on drugs, alcohol, and food; exercise; dress well; groom yourself; and smile, you may have better opportunity to appeal to your dream lover. These are point producing actions which not only add to your appeal, but contribute even more to your attractiveness.

4. *Honesty.* Learn to be honest with yourself and honest with others. Do not boast that you are someone you are not. This not only costs points, but it has another negative side affect. You will never know if someone is attracted to you for what you profess to be or for what you really are. All such deceit will only lead to unhappiness. You must decide that you will be less unhappy if you tell the truth and are found wanting, than if you attract people through deceit. More people will be genuinely attracted to you when you are honest about yourself. Add that you are more comfortable without a facade, and you have a double benefit to being honest. Consider the points you gain for being honest, and you have a triple benefit. Honesty is indeed the best policy.

There is another aspect of honesty that you must address. You must be open and clear about your needs. We all have a desire to be wanted, needed, and loved. In fact romance probably encompasses all three of these components in its package. Do not feign absolute independence. It is not true and will only repel a potential mate. Allow her to know she fulfills a need in your life. You not only want her and love her, but you need her as well. Let her know she can contribute to your life as you can contribute to hers.*

5. *Values.* Be clear about your beliefs and values. To be nebulous will only mean you will attract nebulous people into your life. Decide to become clear on your values if you are ever to attract someone whom you can value. Most of your current values can be represented to you by the company

---

*Author's note: While the feminine case is used in many of these sentences, it is not meant to be sexist. It is used strictly to improve the flow of the sentences. Imagine how awkward it would be if each sentence were to use him and her, or he and she.

you are keeping. Your friends and role models reflect your life. WE GET WHAT WE BELIEVE WE DESERVE. Based on your values, you deserve the friends you have. Observe them. Do they reflect what you want to be? They certainly reflect what you are.

Be aware that your friendships change to reflect changes in you and your point values. As you progress, your relationships with your current friends will change. The bond will be strengthened with those who have the qualities you are gaining. You will drift away from those with whom you are no longer compatible.

Evaluate your friendships to determine your current values and beliefs.

6. *Role Models.* Determine any traits you would like to acquire and which you believe will be valuable in attracting a lover. Observe successful relationships and evaluate the reasons for their success. You can even evaluate failed relationships to determine the reasons for the failure. Ask questions and listen carefully. Most people are willing to discuss their relationships—even if they have failed.

Now that you have determined the characteristics you have and those you need, get to work. You surely have identified enough tasks to keep you occupied. Do not go about this enterprise in a glum manner, as it will only defeat your efforts. Instead relish the growth you are achieving. If the rewards come slowly, be of good cheer. The longer it takes, the higher your self-esteem. The higher your self-esteem, the greater your romance will be. Gain points. Once you believe you are worthy, you will surely attract your mate.

Maintaining a Healthy Relationship

Once you have realized the romance of your dreams, your task is not ended. You must continue to generate points for yourself, and you must continually infuse points into the relationship. Great loves, like great people, can wilt through neglect.

Most unhappiness, separation, and divorce are directly attributable to lost points. One or both partners fails to refresh the partnership with value and nurturing. They take it for granted and assume it will last forever with no further effort on their part. Consequently, this lack of freshness and support results in a loss of interest for the once inseparable companions. This then results in feelings of emptiness and lack which, of course, leads to a loss of points and lower self-esteem for both partners. Eventually the former lovers realize they are unhappy. The once great romance ends.

It needn't happen that way. If you are blessed with a loving relationship, remember to treat it well. Like your own self-image, the relationship needs attention. Positive actions result in points, and points improve everything.

Let me tell you a portion of my story which indicates what can happen if you fail to maintain a healthy relationship and a healthy self-image.

A Personal Story

I was once in love. I loved her as much as I was capable of loving anyone at the time. I had been in love before, but this one affected me more than all the others combined. I would dream of her even while she slept beside me. I thought of her often during my day. Many times I would stop after work to buy her flowers and champagne just because I loved her so much. In my mind we had the love of the century, if not of the ages. She represented everything I wanted from life, and I was content. I no longer had to seek love, for I had found it. I now could focus on other pursuits.

She left me, and I was devastated. It was at once the worst and best thing that has ever happened to me. It was the worst because I lost the most important person in my life. It was the best because *I* had to now become the most important person in my life. I came to realize that I am incapable of loving others if I cannot first love myself. She had left me because I had become incapable of demonstrating the love I felt in my heart.

There is a song that has been recorded by Willie Nelson and a host of others called "You Were Always On My Mind." Until I found out it was a best seller, I thought it had been written especially for me—it so matched my situation. The song begins, "Maybe I didn't love you quite as often as I could have." That fit me well. Though I thought of loving her often, I rarely expressed my love in ways she could appreciate. After she left, I realized that over two years had elapsed since I had brought her flowers or even told her that I loved her. I even forgot her birthday during our last year together. In my mind we were living the romance of the century; in reality we were struggling to even be civil to each other.

I blamed job pressures, economic setbacks, a high mortgage, even other people for my failed romance. The truth was that while I once had enough self-esteem to attract such a wonderful woman to me, I had become complacent. I stopped gaining points for myself or providing them to my relationship. Indeed, as my actions lowered my self-esteem, I found I was less and less able to contribute to our relationship. In fact, the less I was able to love myself, the less I was able to express the love I felt for her. Even then, I was oblivious to the wreakage I was causing. I continued to believe I had our relationship to sustain me. Were I more alert, I would have realized that I was jeopardizing the very thing I valued most and the only thing which was able to create esteem in my life. I failed in my bargain to love her, and she left.

As a result of my loss, my self-esteem was lowered in every area. Because I didn't know what to do, I took actions which cost even more points. As I lost more and more, my self-image became increasingly tarnished. As my self-worth plummeted, I became more cantankerous and antisocial. I thought I was covering my unhappiness, but, of course, I was not.

It is impossible to cover low self-esteem for long. My boss asked me to resign. Six months before, he had given me the highest raise he had ever granted anyone. He indicated the reason wasn't a failure to do quality work, although even that was decidedly becoming suspect. It was instead that my presence in the office was no longer acceptable. I had become morose and argumentative and had lost the very charm which had once made me a valuable employee.

I found another job, but one for which I was unsuited. My point loss was getting to me again. I accepted a position, not because it was what I wanted, but because it was the one I believed I deserved. The job did nothing to nurture me. In fact, I hated it. Being alone and with a job I hated, I was continuing to lose more points, although I was unaware of this. At that time it never occurred to me that there even was such a thing as self-esteem points. It did not matter that I was ignorant, the effect was the same—my life was becoming unbearable. I demonstrated that in every aspect. It was inevitable that I would get negative results.

Long after she left me, I stayed in the shadows of life. My work suffered as much as I did. My social life dwindled to evenings of watching television with a bottle of scotch and a pack of cigarettes, while my only remaining friend, my golden retriever, lay curled near my feet. My bottom occurred then. I felt utterly alone and abandoned. In sheer desperation, I reached out to my neighbors—my first attempt to find a support group. These kind and loving people introduced me to others who were caring and compassionate. I soon felt accepted and this enabled me to heal.

I, who had amassed several lifetimes worth of negative points, was now able to reverse the cycle. I began taking care of myself and my surroundings. I soon made more new friends and felt encouraged to improve my life. I was motivated to take courses and read books to enhance my life even more. As I related in the first chapter, I eventually felt confident enough to start my own business which in turn led to my discovery of the philosophy of points.

I never want to repeat this process again. While it was a valuable learning experience, it was much too painful. Therefore I continue to work at gaining points so my life improves and I need never feel that much despair again.

Steps to Nurturing a Romance

If you are involved in a loving relationship, please avoid my mistakes. Concentrate on improving it even more and you will find it can be the basis for all other growth and happiness. A nurturing relationship can support you while you achieve more and more of the greatness you are meant to enjoy. If you are to realize these benefits, you must sustain and nourish your relationship and your mate as well. If you are blessed with children, you must offer them the same consideration.

Here then are suggestions for nurturing your relationship.

1. *Give.* Look to what you can give to your relationship and your children. If you feel unloved and unappreciated, consider your giving as a form of investment. Everything you give to your family will be returned to you a hundred-fold.

   Put every effort into making your relationship and family better and your bonds with them stronger. Do not measure the contribution of your mate, nor compare your commitment with his. Enjoy what you can give, and be grateful for your capacity to do so.

2. *Be Honest.* Be honest in all aspects of your relationship. Express your feelings. Be considerate of your mate's feelings as well. Be honest but avoid destructive comments. Apologize when you are wrong. Share your joys and your goals. Allow your family to support you in your endeavors. This means being honest about what you are doing, thinking, and feeling. It strengthens your relationship to share the trials as well as the triumphs.

3. *Say Yes.* Practice sharing what it is you like about your mate and your children. Say yes whenever possible. By the time a child is fifteen he has heard the word "No" over 50,000 times. Don't capriciously contribute more "No's" to your mate and your children. Be encouraging. The results will amaze you.

4. *Invest Time.* Schedule time for your relationship. You sought it for so long and with so much energy. Take the time to now sustain, nurture, and enjoy it.

5. *Be Supportive.* You want the best for your mate and children. In fact, you probably believe you know exactly what is best for them. Surprise! Even if you know better, you must allow your loved ones room to explore. They need to know they have your support to try new things regardless of whether they fail or succeed. This is a part of any growth process. Allow them to gain points from their experiences by being supportive and non-judgmental.

6. *Express Your Love and Happiness.* Never, never take your relationship for granted. Express your love and happiness. Use the words as well as the gestures. Gifts and support are fine. Saying "I love you," is supreme.

CHAPTER SUMMARY

1. WE GET WHAT WE BELIEVE WE DESERVE in relationships as well as in every other aspect of life.

2. To attract a loving relationship make yourself more attractive.

3. Gain enough points and love will find you.

4. Learn to love those with whom you now have relationships.

5. Know your values and look to others for values which are important in a successful relationship. Cultivate those values.

6. Once you have achieved a successful relationship, you must continue to develop and nurture it.

7. Give to the relationship and it will grow and sustain you.

9

Special Situations

EVERYONE ENCOUNTERS SPECIAL SITUATIONS in their lives. Some are pleasant and some are not. In either instance there is the opportunity to gain or lose points. Here are some suggestions to help you maximize your point gain and minimize any losses when encountering an extraordinary event. Many of the suggestions are repeated in different categories. Use whatever you can, and be aware of the points resulting from your actions.

Death of a Loved One

1. Grieve, cry, and experience your emotions. It is not healthy to suppress your feelings of loss. You lose points by acting as if the experience was not important enough to be sad, disappointed, or hurt. That is effectively telling your subconscious that you don't matter enough to have had a loving relationship. You do matter! Now prove it by releasing the emotions you've pent up.

If you avoid releasing your emotions, they will manifest themselves regardless. You will lose sleep, become ill, act irrationally, or fail at something which is important to you. You gain positive points by respecting your feelings.

Release your emotions through healthy outlets. Don't get drunk, eat seventy-seven pounds of chocolate, have an affair, or hibernate. Instead, share your feelings with an understanding friend or counselor.

2. Reflect on the good memories you have of the deceased. Remember the value this person had in your life. Being remembered by others is a form of eternal life.

3. Use this as an opportunity to come to terms with your own death.

4. Help others. Take the time to work with others who can use your help. There are hundreds of opportunities to be of service to others. You will gain points and remove the focus from your own problems.

5. Become involved in healthy activities which make you feel good. Clean house, take up golf, paint a picture, take a class, or do any activity that is healthy and will give you positive points. Once again, remember to avoid destructive activities such as overdrinking.

Divorce

1. Grieve, cry, and experience your emotions. It is not healthy to suppress your feelings of loss. You lose points by acting as if the experience was not important enough to be sad,

disappointed, or hurt. That is effectively telling your sub-conscious that you don't matter enough to have had a loving relationship. You do matter! Now prove it by releasing the emotions you've pent up.

If you avoid releasing your emotions, they will mani-fest themselves regardless. You will lose sleep, become ill, act irrationally, or fail at something which is important to you. You gain positive points by respecting your feelings.

Release the emotions through healthy outlets. Don't get drunk, eat seventy-seven pounds of chocolate, have an affair, or hibernate. Instead, share your feelings with an understanding friend or counselor.

2. Be respectful of the other person and of the former relation-ship. You insult yourself, and gather negative points, by finding fault with the other person. After all you are the one who chose or accepted your mate. Esteem him or her, regardless of the faults. You esteem yourself in the process.

3. Do an honest appraisal of the causes of the breakup. Deter-mine where you are at fault so that you may correct your flaws.

4. Pray and cheer for your former mate's future success. Wish for the other person all that you want for yourself. Pray for them to be blessed with health, happiness, prosperity, and love. If you don't believe in prayer, do it anyhow. Pray "To Whom It May Concern" if necessary. Do this for twenty-one consecutive days and you will be amazed at the result. By doing this you gain positive points by telling your subconscious that you are so worthy of good that you can wish it for the one from whom you are estranged.

5. Make a list of how your life will be once you are emotionally free. Write of all the activities you can now do as a result of your new status. You can travel, stay up late, select your own television programs, take classes, meet new people, lose weight, buy new clothes, eat what you like, and generally account only to yourself. Include how you will feel once you are past the hurt. Redefine your goals for five years, one year, and one month. Begin living this way NOW! Don't wait until you are "over it." Build positive points by quickly becoming involved with your new lifestyle. Use the "mini-victories" technique to build confidence and momentum.

6. Rearrange your environment. If you are still living where you were during the relationship, change it to better suit you. Personalize it and make it your own. The process will be therapeutic and the results will please you.

7. Help others. Take the time to work with others who can use your help. There are hundreds of opportunities to be of service to others. You will gain positive points and remove the focus from your own problems.

8. Become involved in healthy activities which make you feel good. Clean house, take up golf, paint a picture, take a class, or do any activity that is healthy and will give you positive points. Once again, avoid destructive activities such as overdrinking, overeating, or promiscuity.

9. List all the reasons you have to feel good about yourself.

10. Visualize yourself being loved.

Unemployment

1. Remain active and avoid thinking of your plight. This is a time when your confidence wanes and you can accumulate a number of negative points. You are not earning an income and are probably having financial problems. Keep active. If you are seeking employment, set a definite schedule for sending resumés, calling prospective employers, answering want ads, and networking with friends and associates. You should arise at the same time each day and follow your normal pre-work rituals such as showering and brushing your teeth. Maintain your discipline.

2. Do a career inventory. List everything you've ever liked about your work. Identify your accomplishments. What are your best skills and personality traits? Does your resumé reflect these assets? List everything you've disliked about your work. Is there a way to avoid these difficulties in the future? What problems have you had in your career? How can you correct them?

   Determine if there are any educational or skill gaps in your repertoire. Can you use this time to increase your marketability? What hobbies do you have that can apply to your career?

   Review the inventory. Are you happy with your chosen field? Did you choose the field or did you happen upon it? What would you rather do? Why don't you do it? You are not too old, nor do you have too many responsibilities to begin again.

   If you are unemployed and want to work or want to change careers but are afraid, it only means that you lack enough self-esteem. Determine where you have a point deficit and take the actions necessary to acquire enough positive points to compensate.

3. Find outlets to maintain your self-esteem. Take special care to accumulate positive points to compensate for those you usually acquired on the job. No matter how much you disliked your job or your boss, you still picked up some positive points. You had the discipline to get up and to show up. You brought home a paycheck. You performed some type of service. Even if you did not think these were much, they did establish some self-worth.

   Now you must compensate for the loss of these positive points. Do so by completing any projects you have been postponing. Clean your garage, write letters, contact old friends, paint your house, or tune your car. Do anything that will make you feel good about yourself.

4. Avoid destructive behavior. Don't stay up until three in the morning watching television and then sleep until noon. Don't get drunk. Don't do anything that will compound your already shaky self-image. Once you start this behavior, it will be very difficult to reverse it.

5. Stand tall and look people in the eye. It is easy to become depressed when unemployed. This can have a detrimental impact on your appearance. Without being aware of it, your shoulders may sag and you will slouch. You may have a difficult time making eye contact. Stop this behavior. Make a conscious effort to stand erect and look at people when you address them. You will notice that you feel better when you do this, and your attitude will improve.

6. Use affirmations and visualization. Write positive affirmations about work. For example you may say, "I am gainfully
   employed as a _____. My salary is $_____, which is
   more than I have ever made. I am happy on my job and my
   employers are very pleased with the quality and quantity
   of my work." Repeat this affirmation at least twenty times
   a day.

   Take time to visualize a great job. Picture yourself
   going to work. See what you are wearing. Imagine your
   work place and your co-workers. See yourself performing
   your job. Look at your paycheck and smile.

Financial Crisis

1. Maintain your integrity. Remember who you are and what
   values you possess. Do not compromise your long-term
   self-esteem to extricate yourself from a temporary situation.

2. Evaluate positive means to weather the crisis. It is better
   to find ways to earn more money than it is to reduce
   spending, although both may be necessary.

3. It may be that your lack of self-esteem brought you to the
   crisis. If so, concentrate on gaining points. The gains you
   make to your self-worth will have the double benefit of
   providing you with the internal resources to lead you out
   of the crisis and reducing the possibility of it recurring.

4. Use your support group for guidance, comfort, and opportunity. They may well be able to offer you suggestions and
   may also be able to share their own similar experiences.

Starting a New Job

1. Maintain your discipline. Continue to exercise, eat properly, and take adequate rest. You may wish to devote all of your resources to the new job, but it is important that you keep a perspective.

2. Do something extra at work. It will help your career immensely if you establish yourself as a quality worker. Prove your abilities and you will gain respect. This will create an environment in which you can thrive. In other words, invest a lot of points early in your new job and they will compound for you.

3. Avoid all tendencies to feel smug, complacent, arrogant, or superior. No matter how spectacular your new job, you will function best if you are gracious and grateful.

4. Do not make enemies, but build alliances. Remember, friends come and friends go, but enemies accumulate. Avoid causing resentment in someone who may harm you later and will relish the opportunity to do so.

5. Continue to build self-esteem points with your work so you may qualify and feel worthy of an even higher position.

Moving

1. Organize your surroundings as quickly and as well as possible. Strive to feel comfortable with your new environment.

2. Make a point to meet your new neighbors and strive to feel a part of your community.

3. Do something to reflect a high degree of self-esteem. Plant flowers, add paint or wallpaper, hang paintings, or clean thoroughly.

4. Use the move as an opportunity to break old negative habits. If you dropped your clothes on the floor each night, now hang and fold them properly. If you ate in front of the TV, dine to soft music.

5. View the move as an opportunity to cultivate new positive habits. Walk after dinner or rise early to exercise. Set aside a special place in your new surroundings in which you can meditate and relax. Sell all your TV's save one and buy books.

Quitting a Job

1. Maintain your dignity. Even if you have been mistreated or harassed on your job, do not lower yourself to your employer's level.

2. Refuse to accept abuse. If your employer labels you ungrateful or worse, you can quietly yet forcefully indicate you do not deserve such treatment.

3. Do not unnecessarily make any enemies. By rising above any pettiness from your employer or co-workers you will gain self-esteem points. It is also possible you will meet

some of these people at a different time and place. Leave
open the possibility that they may be kind or helpful in
the future.

4. No matter how bad the conditions or how much you want
   to leave, make sure you receive all the compensation you
   have earned. Do not do anything or fail to do anything
   which will cause you resentment and point loss in the
   future.

Handling a Difficult Boss

1. Maintain your dignity. Even if you have been mistreated
   or harassed on your job, do not lower yourself to your
   employer's level.

2. Dig deep within yourself and find the courage to confront
   your boss. Determine what your problems are and explore
   possible solutions. Even though you may not be calm, keep
   your anger in check and avoid shouting. Express your views
   and listen to his.

3. If there is a resolution, work to maintain all agreements
   you have made.

Firing Someone

1. Become clear in your mind on the reason for the termina-
   tion.

2. Have the meeting in private. If possible, provide an exit for the terminated employee where he doesn't have to face his co-workers. If that is not possible, give him time to compose himself before asking him to leave.

3. Present your point of view clearly and without malice or superiority. Allow the other person to maintain his dignity.

4. If he yells, screams, or cusses, remain calm. He may be upset, but you will only lose points if you become that way too.

5. Firing someone is not easy. Be firm and dignified and you will gain self-esteem points for having the courage to handle such a difficult task with aplomb.

Handling Difficult People on the Job

1. Be it boss, co-worker, or employee, you need not accept abuse from anyone. Before you initiate a confrontation, however, determine if there is something about you which attracts such abuse. Do you wear an "Abuse Me" sign? If so, resolve to change yourself.

2. To the degree you are capable, be loving and understanding of the abuser. He may suffer from low self-esteem and be incapable of regular appropriate behavior. This does not mean you need condone or tolerate such abuse however. You do have a right to fair and equitable treatment.

3. Dig deep within yourself and find the courage to confront the person. Determine what your problems are and explore possible solutions. Even though you may not be calm, keep your anger in check and avoid shouting. Express your views and listen to his. If you feel it is necessary, bring a witness and log the meeting.

4. Discuss your difficulties with your support group. They may be able to aid you with very specific suggestions.

Handling Difficult Tradespeople

1. Regardless of their attitude, title, or point of view, tradespeople work for you. This includes doctors, attorneys, therapists, and even plumbers. Be clear on your needs and wants and do not allow them to exceed your limits of patience, tolerance, or financial considerations.

2. Trust your instincts and act on them. If you feel uncomfortable with any tradesperson, find another. Do not allow yourself to be cheated. It will only lower your self-esteem and make you more susceptible to being cheated in the future.

3. Expect quality service. Put on your "I DESERVE THE BEST" sign and demand they comply.

Difficult People in Social Situations

1. Do you have a sense of humor? Use it when confronted with a boor. Laugh off his insults and return them with amusing

banter. Most obnoxious people use rude behavior to feel superior. Ignore their tactics and they will probably seek another victim.

2. Leave. Unless you are compelled to stay, you need not accept abuse in a social situation. You are presumably there to enjoy yourself. There is no reason to remain if you are not doing so.

3. Confront the jerk. Use this as an opportunity to really gain points. Take a risk and face the fool. Tell him off. Tell him where to go. Regardless of the outcome, you can feel good about yourself for having the courage to face a difficult situation. Be wary of losing yourself in anger, however. It is appropriate to express your opinion, be it positive or negative. It is appropriate to express your disappointment in the actions of another person. It is appropriate to stand your ground. It is not appropriate to lose control, act irrationally, or demean anyone. Confront an irritating person and gain points; explode in anger and you will lose them.

Beginning a New Relationship

1. Maintain your integrity. Even though you wish to impress the other person, avoid bragging and aggrandizement. You will only lose points.

2. Maintain your discipline. Continue to exercise, eat properly, take adequate rest, and work. You may wish to devote all of your resources to the other person. Don't. You will

only create difficulties in your life which will cost you points.

3. Offer positive points to the relationship. Do activities together which are nourishing to both of you. Respect the other person's values and expect respect for yours.

Marriage

1. You have finally arrived. You are now one of two, a partner in a glorious union based on love and mutual respect. Please, please, please do not make this the pinnacle of your relationship. Instead make it the beginning of a lifetime filled with ever-increasing happiness, support, and growth.

2. Establish rituals which re-emphasize your love and trust. Devote a special time for each other. This can be anything from grocery shopping to making love so long as it is your time.

3. Find ways to add points to the relationship. Give all you can to strengthen your bonds. You may well be storing for a difficult time when you need all the love and support your marriage can offer.

4. Make your mate your best friend. Enjoy each other and your life together.

Birth of Children

1. Resolve to endow your child with as many self-esteem points as you are capable of granting. Do this early and often. The messages your child receives now are going to weigh heavily for there are few other messages there to counter them.

2. Resolve to say "YES" more than "NO." You want your child to face life head on, to strive, and to succeed. Saying "YES" will encourage him, saying "NO" will discourage him. Note the word "encourage." You can help your child to face life "in courage" by being supportive and loving.

3. Use this blessed event as an opportunity to rededicate yourself to your spouse and to your other children. Find a way all can gain esteem from your child's birth. It will not only improve your life, but will be a great testimony to your child.

Raising Children

1. Your job as a parent is to train your child to be an adult. This means enforcing loving discipline and exposing him to life in a safe environment.

2. Encourage your child to experiment with career and life options. If he wants to be a fireman one week and a doctor the next, that is fine. Accept his viewpoint and discuss his options with him.

3. Allow your child to profit from your experience by lovingly and openly discussing your life. Tell of your mistakes, triumphs, joys, lessons learned, and lessons ignored. Discuss the perils of drug abuse, alcohol abuse, and promiscuity. Be loving and understanding. Recall your own childhood and treat your child in the manner you wish you had been treated.

4. Be an example. Your child gains or loses more points through observing and copying your actions than he ever will from your words.

Children Leaving Home

1. When one of your children leaves home, you may well feel there is a gap or emptiness in your life. Make sure you fill that spot with some positive activities and thoughts. Shower more love and attention on the rest of your family, take up a hobby, or become more involved with the community.

2. Because your child (even if he is now an adult, he is still your child) is no longer living with you, it does not mean you will lose contact. The relationship is still there; it is just different. Find ways for both of you to gain points from this changed situation. Write, call, and encourage each other.

3. One of the greatest gifts you can give your adult child is to ask his advice. You instill him with points by indicating you value his opinion and are willing to accept his sugges-

tions. For years you taught him, now give him the gift of allowing him to give back to you.

Vacation and Travel

1. Behave yourself. Enjoy yourself, relax, and have fun, but don't use a vacation as an excuse to practice destructive behavior. The point loss is not worth the temporary satisfaction.

2. Take the opportunity to expand your life. Go somewhere new, learn something, meet new people. Any change of scenery and pattern can open new paths in your brain and make you a richer and more enlightened person.

3. Use a vacation to explore life options. Go to a place you may wish live when you retire.

4. Take the opportunity to renew your spirit. Return refreshed, not needing a recovery time.

Retirement

1. Never, ever, retire from anything. Instead begin something new. If it is time to set aside things of the past, such as a job, by all means do so, but make sure you have a plan for your future. Make sure you can handle the freedom and opportunity now available.

2. Avoid ruts. A rut is just a grave with both ends kicked out. Don't waste your golden years vegetating in front of a

television. Instead make the effort to become involved with the myriad of activities available to one who is free of the responsibilities of a career.

3. Do it today. Don't think that because you have the rest of your life you can postpone anything. These are the times you have been waiting for—relish them.

4. Remember all those things you wanted to do, but were too busy? Now you're not too busy, nor are you too old. Think of an activity and there is probably someone older than you doing it. This time in life can be a gift—use it well.

Health Problems

1. Visualize wellness. See yourself as being healthy and feeling energetic.

2. Determine activities you will do as soon as you regain your health. Picture yourself enjoying life.

3. Decide if there was anything you could have done to prevent or reduce your likelihood of experiencing ill-health. Resolve to improve your health habits. Accumulate health points to improve your well-being.

4. Rally the support of friends and family. Accept and experience the love they have for you. Allow them to love you to health.

CHAPTER SUMMARY

1. Regardless of the situation, you can gain self-esteem points by taking positive and appropriate actions.

2. Your relationships with other people are important. Each encounter, regardless of the situation, offers the opportunity to improve your self-esteem.

3. No matter how painful a situation may be, you can make it better if you are willing to make an effort to gain points. By the same token you can always make it worse by falling apart or doing something inappropriate.

4. Remember your every thought and action generates or costs points based upon your efforts. No matter what the event, you control the resulting point score. It is your choice.

10

Be a Winner

THE FIRST LINE OF THIS BOOK makes a distinction between winners and losers. Winners face life head on, accepting whatever comes and relishing the challenge, while losers slink through the shadows trying not to be noticed. Winners have acquired characteristics which enable them to gain an advantage in most situations. Their actions appear to be effortless and natural. As we have learned, they carry enough self-esteem points to be compelled to succeed. They absolutely believe they deserve success and are driven to achieve it.

By contrast, losers are continually encountering difficulties. They seem so unlucky. Their life is peppered with a litany of adversity and misfortune—real and imagined. They can find a way to lose even when victory seems imminent.

You can gain enough self-esteem points to be a winner easily and naturally. All you need do is develop those traits which lend themselves to a fruitful, productive life. You can gain self-esteem from all of your daily activities. You can add to your point total by studying growth-enhancing programs, participating in support group activities, and nurturing your loving relationships. In time you will find you have made remarkable progress. The words of Rene Coue will ring true, "Every day in every way I am getting better and better."

This book has presented a great deal of material on how to gain points and avoid losing them. You learned visualization and meditation techniques to multiply your score. You learned methods to reconcile the past. And, you learned the value of giving and supporting others. If this seems like a lot to handle at once, please remember the basic concept of "points." To have a quality life you must live a quality life. YOU GET WHAT YOU BELIEVE YOU DESERVE.

All you need do to enjoy the benefits of high self-esteem is to *make a decision to lead a life which will enhance that esteem.* From that moment your life will get better and better. Develop a program for living which encompasses these growth principles and you will surely find yourself happier and more fulfilled. In the Big Book of Alcoholics Anonymous there are promises made to those who stay sober and work the 12 Steps:

> If we are painstaking about this phase of our development, we will be amazed before we are half way through. We are going to know a new freedom and a new happiness. We will not regret the past nor wish to shut the door on it. We will comprehend the word serenity and we will know peace. No matter how far down the scale we have gone, we will see how our experience can benefit others. That feeling of uselessness and self-pity will disappear. We will lose interest in selfish things and gain interest in our fellows. Self-seeking will slip away. Our whole attitude and outlook upon life will change. Fear of people and of economic insecurity will leave us. We will intuitively know how to handle situations which used to baffle us . . . (Alcoholic's Anonymous, pp. 83-84).

Doesn't this sound like a marvelous way to live? You have the power and potential to enjoy such a quality life. The people in A.A., and all other programs based on the 12 Steps, learn to lead the type of life which makes these benefits available to them. They are taught to ". . . practice these principles in all affairs." The full text of the twelfth step is: "Having had a spiritual awakening as a result of these steps, we tried to carry this message to other alcoholics, and to practice these principles in all our affairs" (p. 60). If you can practice positive principles in such a manner that you continually gain points, you too will enjoy serenity and peace of mind.

Summary of Points

1. *Do the Right Thing.* The primary principle of life is that your actions are rewarded in kind. Lie, cheat, and steal if you choose, but don't be bewildered if you experience poverty, loneliness, and depression. Instead, do what you know to be right and proper in all situations. Life will reward you a hundredfold for your efforts. Train yourself to be aware of gaining or losing points, and you will choose the proper course of action. You cannot make deals with life. It will brook no games nor manipulations for very long. If you are either cunning or superstitious, you will soon suffer. Be responsible, act responsibly, and reap the rewards. Heed the words of Disraeli, "Principle is ever my motto, not expediency."

2. *Take Responsibility For Your Life.* Winners have the ability to take responsibility for their actions and to accept any situation in which they find themselves. A winner is not a victim. To view yourself as a victim is only detrimental to

your happiness and self-esteem. Victims are easily manip-
ulated by others because they view themselves as powerless.
Guard against wearing the victim's cloak. Every one of us
could tell a tale of how we were cheated, oppressed, de-
ceived, exploited, or used. Don't succumb to any temptation to do so. A winner will refuse to accept the role of
victim; a loser will audition for the part. Refuse to accept
the label of victim. Do not allow others to console you. To
be a winner you must act like one. That means you must
accept responsibility for all your thoughts, words, and
actions regardless of the results they generate. Learn to
control your point of view. Avoid feeling sorry for yourself.
Instead, determine how you can best take advantage of your
current circumstances.

3. *Be Involved.* Winners are involved with life. They do not
spend an inordinate amount of time on self-centered pursuits. A winner is an individual who can learn a self-improvement technique, then immediately practice it. One
example of a loser is a person who is constantly seeking to
enhance his knowledge of life's secrets while never actually
applying them.

A winner finds joy in work, gives to others, freely
shares knowledge, and exploits his talents to the fullest.
Notice the winners. They are the ones who seem to do just
a little more and have a little more energy than the others.
They have the extra energy because they are not wasting it
in constant introspection and self-centered concerns.

To be a winner, find ways to give of yourself. Know
that you have a great deal to give. Remember, "God is able
to provide you with every blessing in abundance, so that
you may always have enough of everything and may provide in abundance for every good work" (II Corinthians

9:8). Share your abundance. Become involved with your community. Take pride in your work and share that pride with your fellow workers. Directly give to others less fortunate than yourself. This means giving of your time and of yourself. It doesn't mean dutifully writing a check to some charitable organization merely to assuage your conscience.

Be a little league coach, a den mother, or a driver for the elderly. Visit a hospital—even if you know no one there, run for local office, recycle. Find ways to save your employer time or money. Take a few seconds to re-inspect your work; take courses to improve your knowledge. Teach a course. If you dedicate your time and efforts to something greater than yourself, you will find the points roll in. You will soon be healthier, happier, and will relish what life has to offer.

4. *Be Positive in Your Speech.* Listen to others speak. Winners pepper their talk with positive statements and their stories are usually of victories and accomplishments—theirs or others.

This doesn't mean you need constantly be a cheerleader or a preacher. A self-effacing sense of humor can be charming and engaging. A winner may tell a tale on himself that is amusing, yet typically there is a positive side to it. He learned something or he is making a point. Often it is to help the listeners avoid a similar pitfall. Christ taught by parable; other winners often teach by anecdote.

Learn to make positive statements: "I learned a great deal," rather than negative ones: "Boy, do I feel like a fool." Avoid bragging and false pride, but learn to emphasize the positive aspects of any situation in your thinking and your speech. Remember, what you say aloud or in your mind is registered as a gain or loss of points in your subconscious mind.

5. *Enjoy the Present Moment.* Have you ever had a peak experience? One that makes you glad to be alive? If so, you were probably so fully engrossed in the present moment you had little consideration for the past or the future. Learn to feel that way always. Pay attention to your surroundings. Lose yourself in the present moment and life will always be a joy.

There is a story of a Zen master who was being chased by a man-eating tiger. He came to a cliff and dove over the side, clinging to a vine as he went. Looking down he noticed there was a man-eating shark swimming in the waters below. Not only that, the vine was pulling loose from the earth. As he hung there, suspended between the tiger and the shark he noticed a patch of strawberries within reach. He picked one, tasted it, and commented, "My isn't this strawberry delicious." Live in the present moment and life will always seem delicious.

6. *Be Willing to Take a Risk.* Raise your emotional thermostat to allow you to burn with passion. Take healthy risks with no consideration for the outcome. Enjoy the exhilaration of the effort and the adventure. It is by taking risks that we expand our capacity to face life head-on. Every risk taken contributes to our growth and our self-esteem.

Each of us is surrounded by our own customized comfort zone. It surrounds us like a protective plastic bubble. Actions you take which fall within your comfort zone are not risky and therefore not emotionally disruptive. Actions which are outside of your comfort zone are, by definition, risky. You are guaranteed to be uncomfortable. The further you venture outside of your comfort zone, the more you feel emotionally unsettled.

Why then, would you want to take risks so you can be sure to be uncomfortable? You do it to expand your comfort zone. If you take a risk once, you will find it easier to do the same action again and again. In fact, that which was once a risk becomes easy and often enjoyable once it is encompassed within your comfort zone.

Your comfort zone expands in all directions with a single risk. If you overcome your stage fright and speak before a large group of people, you will find it easier to ask for a raise or take an adventuresome vacation. On top of that, the points you gain will make it easier to lose that last ten pounds or give up cigarettes.

7. *Strive for Physical, Mental, and Emotional Well-Being.* Without becoming self-centered or obsessed, take action to improve your well-being. Select nutritious foods, groom yourself, and exercise for your physical fitness. Read and take classes to improve your mind. Learn and master techniques to improve your emotional well-being. Take some time each week for each of these endeavors. It will promote your self-esteem and maintain your health.

8. *Practice Balance.* Avoid selective involvement with any activity to the detriment of all other aspects of your life. Practice balance by maintaining healthy interest in your growth and well-being, your family and friends, your career, your environment, your community, your world, and your spiritual affairs. Have goals but avoid obsessions. Learn to adjust your thinking as conditions warrant. Con-

sider others while maintaining and improving the quality of your life.

9. *Relax.* Take time each day to relax and renew your spirit. The aborigines of Australia will periodically stop and remain absolutely still. They do this to allow their souls to catch up to them. You need do the same.

10. *Enjoy Your Life.* No matter what your current circumstance, there are certainly many aspects of your life that are good. Enjoy what you have and be grateful for it. To begin, you are reading this book or having it read to you. That means you have a capacity to comprehend. You can learn. If you can learn, you can improve.

     You can always make a choice to enjoy yourself and to be happy. Accept the circumstances in which you find yourself, choose to be happy, and find ways to enhance your joy. Life is a feast to be relished. Do yourself a favor and enjoy.

Story of a Winner

Let me tell you the story of a winner. Her name is Rita and she is ninety years of age. She lives across the street from my parents in a retirement community in Arizona. She is widowed, lives on a limited income, and is, of course, old by most standards. Yet she enjoys life and is involved with others. Her home is immaculate and she is always starting new projects. Last time I saw her she had carpeted her garage with remnants salvaged from the trash of a local carpet store. She is always cooking for others in the neighborhood and can often be seen helping with their landscaping. She even sawed down a small tree in my parents' yard because it was infested with insects. She bowls twice a week and occasionally rides a charter bus all night to Laughlin, Nevada where she plays the slot machines all day using money she saved from recycling cans, bottles, and news-papers. She then rides back on the bus the next night. She has a wonderful sense of humor and appears to have all her faculties. She is a joy to meet and to know.

Rita typifies the winner traits identified here. She refuses to see herself as a victim, even though she misses her husband and would like to be able to leave Arizona during the scorching summer. She makes the very best of her situation. She does not sit home to deal with her depression or her aches and pains. Instead she is involved with her life, her property, and her community. She rightfully points with pride to her accomplish-ments, and her stories reflect on a happy and joyous life. She enjoys herself and looks forward to her trips to Laughlin and to the people she will meet. I suspect the people on the bus and even the cynical casino operators look forward to seeing her too. The world is truly better for having Rita here. She is a winner.

Be a winner as well. Remember, you choose your life through your thoughts and actions. Choose wisely and live well. Come out from those shadows and relish all that life has to offer.

References

Alcoholics Anonymous. Alcoholics Anonymous World Service, Inc. p. 60.

Allen, James. (1959). *As a Man Thinketh.* Peter Pauper Press, Inc.

Bacon, Francis. (1625). Of Studies. *Essays.*

Brandon, Nathaniel. (1969). *The Psychology of Self-Esteem.* Nash Publishing Corp.

Cousins, Norman (1979). *Anatomy of an Illness as Perceived by the Patient.* New York: Norton.

Dewey, John (1947). Morals and Conduct. In *The World's Great Thinkers.* New York: Random House.

Eliot, George. (1874) *Daniel Deronda.* Book 2, chapter 13.

Emerson, Ralph Waldo (1947). Compensation. In *The World's Great Thinkers.* New York: Random House.

Epictetus (1947). The Manual. Number 8. In *The World's Great Thinkers.* New York: Random House.

Epicurus (1947). Principle Doctrines. Number V. In *The World's Great Thinkers.* New York: Random House.

Farber, Don & Fields, Rick. (1988). *Taking Refuge in L.A.: Life in a Vietnamese Buddhist Temple.* Aperture.

Fox, Emmet (1938). *The Sermon on the Mount.* Harper & Row.

Franklin, Benjamin (1758). *Poor Richard's Almanack.*

Hill, Napoleon (1960). *Think and Grow Rich.* Fawcett Crest.

James, William (1980). *Principles of Psychology,* 2 vols. Dover.

Maltz, Maxwell (1960). *Psych-Cybernetics.* Prentice-Hall.

Peale, Norman Vincent (1986). *Why Some Positive Thinkers Get Powerful Results.* Oliver Nelson Books.

Prather, Hugh (1977). *Notes on Love and Courage.* Doubleday.

Robbins, Anthony (1989). *Personal Power. A 30-Day Program for Unlimited Success.* Robbins Research International, audio tapes.

Siegal, Bernie S. (1986). *Love, Medicine, and Miracles.* New York: Harper & Row.

Simonton, O. Carl, Matthews-Simonton, Stephanie & Creighton, James (1980). *Getting Well Again.* Bantam Books.

Thoreau, Henry David. (1854). *Walden.* AMS Press.

Thurber, James (1969). The Secret Life of Walter Mitty. *My World and Welcome To It.* New York: Harbrace.

Watts, Alan W. (1957). *The Way of Zen.* New York: Vintage.

Webster's Dictionary (1962). Little & Ives.

Appendix A:
Alcoholics Anonymous
12 Step Program of Recovery

THE FOLLOWING ARE THE 12 steps of Alcoholics Anonymous. These same steps are used as a basis for hundreds of other support and recovery programs. Note that only the first and last steps mention anything about alcohol. The rest dictate a healthy approach to clearing the wreckage of the past.

1. We admitted we were powerless over alcohol and our lives had become unmanageable.

2. Came to believe that a Power greater than ourselves could restore us to sanity.

3. Made a decision to turn our will and our lives over to the care of God as we understood Him.

4. Made a searching and fearless inventory of ourselves.

5. Admitted to God, to ourselves, and to another human being the exact nature of our wrongs.

6. Were entirely ready to have God remove all these defects of character.

7. Humbly asked him to remove our shortcomings.

8. Made a list of all persons we had harmed, and became willing to make amends to them all.

9. Made direct amends to such people wherever possible, except when to do so would injure them or others.

10. Continued to take personal inventory and when we were wrong promptly admitted it.

11. Sought through prayer and meditation to improve our conscious contact with God as we understood Him, praying only for knowledge of His will for us and the power to carry it out.

12. Having had a spiritual awakening as a result of these steps, we tried to carry this message to alcoholics, and to practice these principles in all our affairs.

Appendix B
Support Groups

MOST OF THESE GROUPS ARE LISTED in your local telephone directory. You may also contact your local public library for assistance in locating a group of interest to you.

Most of these groups are free and are supported by contributions. There is usually no membership requirement other than a desire to join.

Adult Children of Alcoholics (ACA)—to learn to deal with the difficulties of growing up in an alcoholic household.

Al-Anon—for support in dealing with loved ones who are alcoholic.

Alcoholics Anonymous (AA)—for help in stopping drinking and learning to live well without alcohol.

Alzheimers Support Group—to support those with a loved one suffering from Alzheimers.

American Legion—an organization supporting American values.

American Mothers Inc.—a support group for mothers of all ages.

Benevolent Paternal Order of Elks (BPOE)—a paternal organization concerned with community issues and charitable works.

Big Brothers/Big Sisters—an organization where adults become a friend to a fatherless or motherless child.

Cancer Support Group—a support group for those with cancer by those who also suffer from it.

Chamber of Commerce—an associaton of local business and communitiy leaders and those concerned about their community.

Cocaine Anonymous (CA)—for help in stopping cocaine usage and living without it.

Clutterers Anonymous—for those who just can't seem to get organized and whose life is literally a mess.

Codependents Anonymous (CODA)—for help with issues related to difficulties in dealing with other people or placing too much reliance on other people.

Democratic Party—a political group supporting Democratic candidates and issues.

Fraternal Order of Eagles—a fraternal organization for those concerned with community issues.

Lions Club—an organization concerend with local charitable and health issues.

Mothers Against Drunk Driving (MADD)—a group for those interested in reducing drunken driving and a support group for those who are victims of drunken drivers.

Narcotics Anonymous (NA)—for help in quitting drugs and living without the need for them.

Neurotics Anonymous (NA)—for help in coping with life and its daily problems.

Overeaters Anonymous (OA)—for help with food addictions and compulsive eating disorders.

Parents Anonymous—for dealing with the difficulties of child rearing.

Parents Without Partners (PWP)—a social and support organization for single parents.

Rational Recovery—an alcoholic recovery program without any emphasis on spiritual issues.

Republican Party—a political group supporting Republican candidates and issues.

Salvation Army—a religious organization concerned with the less fortunate among us.

Sierra Club—for those concerned with enviromental issues.

Students Against Drunk Driving (SADD)—for young people opposed to the ravages caused by drunk and drug impaired drivers.

Sex Addicts Anonymous (SAA)—for help in dealing with compulsive sexual behavior.

Shoppers Anonymous—for help in dealing with compulsive spending habits.

Smokers Anonymous—for help in stopping smoking and living without tobacco.

Take Off Pounds Sensibly (TOPS)—for help in losing weight by changing your habits.

Toastmasters International—to learn to improve your public speaking ability.

ToughLove—a support group for those who can't seem to say no to their loved ones.

Veterans of Foreign Wars (VFW)—a support organization for those who have served in American wars or police actions.

Vietnam Vets Reunited—a support group for those who served in Vietnam and were traumatized by it.

Weightwatchers—for help in losing weight and keeping it off.

Appendix C
Suggested Reading List

THE FOLLOWING SUGGESTED READING LIST is quite short. While there are many other excellent books on goal achievement, there are few on improving self-esteem. It is, of course, more important to increase your self-esteem through action than it is to attempt to improve it by reading books. Read less and live more. The results will be better.

Flow, The Psychology of Optimal Experience by Mihaly Csikszent-mihalyi. New York: HarperCollier, 1991.

Psycho-Cybernetics by Maxwell Maltz. Wilshire.

The Seven Habits of Highly Effective People by Stephen Covey. New York: Simon & Schuster, 1989.

The Sermon on the Mount: The Key to Success in Life by Emmet Fox.
New York: HarperCollins, 1989.

Think and Grow Rich by Napoleon Hill. New York: Fawcett
Crest, 1987.